Tea

A Very British Beverage

Paul Chrystal

Paul Chrystal was educated at the universities of Hull and Southampton, where he took degrees in Classics. He has worked in medical publishing for thirty-five years but now combines this with writing features for national newspapers, as well as appearing regularly on BBC local radio and on the BBC World Service. He is the author of some thirty books on a wide range of subjects, including histories of York and other northern places, the Rowntree family, the social history of chocolate, and various aspects of classical literature and history. He drinks a modest six cups of tea a day, is married with three children and lives in York.

First published 2014

Amberley Publishing
The Hill, Stroud
Gloucestershire, GL5 4EP

www.amberley-books.com

British Library Cataloguing in Publication Data.
A catalogue record for this book is available from the British Library.

ISBN 978 1 4456 3349 7
Ebook ISBN 978 1 4456 3360 2

Typeset in 9.5pt on 12.5pt Sabon.
Typesetting and Origination by Amberley Publishing.
Printed in the UK.

Contents

Camellia sinensis, the tea plant, from a late nineteenth-century print. This is what this book is all about ...

Introduction

The ubiquitous cup of tea is as much a part of British life as indifferent weather, the BBC or the queue at the post office. Tea, since its arrival here in the seventeenth century, has shaped our lives, our history, our work, our culture and even our bodies. Not surprisingly for a drink that we take throughout the day, every day, there is a fascinating story to tell about its origins and how it took Britain by storm to become our second most popular beverage after tap water.

Britain has an intimate love affair with tea; tea has an intimate love affair with Britain: look at the facts. On average we each drink three and a half cups of tea every day, or 130,000 tonnes in a year, 96 per cent of which are from tea bags. We Britons drink 165 million cups per day and 62 billion cups per year; 70 per cent of the population (over age ten) drank tea yesterday; over 25 per cent of all the milk consumed in the UK goes into your cup of tea. In the two minutes or so it has taken me to type these two paragraphs, the tea-ometer on the Tea Council UK website has clocked up a staggering 191,000 cups of tea consumed in the UK; 70 million cups have been made today so far, by 11 a.m.

This book begins with a short survey of the early history of tea; it then goes on to chart its development as something quintessentially British as it slowly but surely insinuated itself into our culture, language and society: afternoon tea, tea gardens, tea dances, Lyons teahouses, teatime, tea breaks, tea for two, storms in tea cups and builders' tea are all described and explored. Our loss of the American colonies, the Opium Wars, votes for women, victory in the two world wars and tea in the 'Troubles' all owe something to a nice cup of tea. English literature mentions tea and teatime all the time; the Beatles and the Rolling Stones all take tea.

The story of our intimate relationship with tea is in effect the social history of Britain, reflecting aspects of the nation's trade, manners, fashion, culture, drinking habits, industrial legislation, foreign policy, and its health. *Tea: A Very British Beverage* tells that fascinating story, describing how tea has defined us and informed our way of life over the last 500 years. Like Samuel Johnson, we just can't get enough of it: 'You cannot make tea so fast as I can gulp it down.' So, put the kettle on, and read on ...

Tea cups and saucers dating from 1885 in a Crown Derby Porcelain Company catalogue.

1

Where it All Started: All the Tea in China, and Japan

China

Once upon a time, when the Emperor Shen Nung was travelling to a far-flung province, he and his entourage stopped for a break, the world's very first tea break as it turned out. Shen Nung, a scientist, knew how important it was to boil all drinking water; accordingly, the servants began to boil the water as they sat in a grove of *Camellia sinensis* trees. The place was central China; the date was 2737 BC, around the same time as the Egyptians started work on the pyramids of Giza. That day, however, was to be very special: a gentle breeze blew some leaves from the *Camellia sinensis* into the emperor's cauldron of water; Shen Nung then took a sip of what was to be the world's first cup of tea. He liked it, it caught on, took the name 'tea' and has become one of the most celebrated and serendipitous discoveries the world has known. But it was not just the trajectory of the breeze-blown leaves that was fortuitous; Shen Nung happened to be a noted herbalist. Nothing if not dedicated to his work, he personally tested thousands of medicinal herbs, some of which were poisonous; his legendary transparent body allowed him to see at first-hand the pharmacodynamic effects of each experimentation. He went on to use his newly discovered tea as an antidote to seventy or so toxic herbs. But tea could not save him from the fatal effect of his final experiment. One herb turned out to be particularly toxic: he ate it, and his intestines exploded. Shen Nung is now revered as the father of Chinese medicine and the discoverer of tea.

An alternative legend champions Bodhidharma as the discoverer; he was an Indian prince who embraced Zen Buddhism and in the sixth century BC travelled to China to spread the faith. Meditation could be a twenty-four-hour occupation so Bodhidharma chewed tea leaves as a stimulant to keep him awake. Another legend says that Bodhidharma, not unreasonably, fell asleep after meditating in front of a wall for nine years and angrily cut off his eyelids to prevent a recurrence. The discarded lids grew into the first tea plant: 'Cast to the ground, the severed eyelids grew into a tea plant which, when brewed, could banish sleep!'

At first tea was made in slabs: green and black tea leaves were beaten and fashioned into brick shapes and dried. To make a drink of tea, some of the brick was simply grated off and boiled in water to form a mortar, and the result would then be mixed with other herbs, ginger and orange.

Monkey pluckers: enlisting angry monkeys in the harvesting of tea in China. 'Monkey-picked tea' (Ma nau mi ti kuan yin) is still available: *Rare Wild Chinese Tea; Picked Only by Specially Trained Monkeys; Contains Powerful Antioxidants.*

Tea production in China. On display at Bettys Café Tea Rooms in Stonegate, York.

Tea bricks were a viable currency due to the high value of tea throughout China, Tibet, Mongolia and Central Asia, just as salt bricks were in parts of Africa and chocolate was in Mesoamerica. Indeed, tea bricks were the currency of choice over metallic coins among the nomads of Mongolia and Siberia. Tea bricks were still used as an edible currency in Siberia until the end of the Second World War. There are many stories surrounding the harvesting of tea, one of which concerns a village in which monkeys pick the tea: the villagers stand below the monkeys and aggravate them; the monkeys get angry, grab handfuls of tea leaves and throw them down at the villagers.

Serendipity and tea does not end with Shen Nung. Not long after the discovery of tea, the Chinese empress Leizu chanced upon silkworms during a midday bowl of tea when a cocoon fell into her tea. The hot water had the effect of unwrapping the silk until it stretched across her garden. She acquired a grove of mulberry trees and domesticated the worms that made the cocoons; Leizu is credited with inventing the silk reel and the silk loom.

Japan

An itinerant Japanese Buddhist monk, Dengyo Daishi, took tea tree seeds home with him during the Sui Dynasty (AD 589–618): tea drinking soon became an integral part of Japanese culture, played out on a daily basis in the tea ceremony. In 1191, Myoan Eisai (1141–1215), the Zen priest, took tea seeds home to Kyoto after a visit to China to study religion and philosophy; in 1211 he wrote the first book on tea in Japan, *Kissa Yōjōki*, or *How to Stay Healthy by Drinking Tea*. It opens with the profound endorsement: 'Tea is

A page from the 28 May 1905 *Detroit Free Press* showing and describing various aspects of cherry blossom time in Japan, including a teahouse garden. Those 'little brown people' were, of course, to come back and haunt the Americans around thirty-five years later.

An eighteenth-century woodblock Japanese print depicting a typically elegant porcelain bowl and lacquer-ware saucer. Courtesy of Jane Pettigrew.

'Matrons, who toss the cup, and see / The grounds of fate in grounds of tea / The bitter dregs of fortune's cup to drain.' Alexander Pope (1688–1744)

the ultimate mental and medical remedy and has the ability to make one's life more full and complete.'

In the sixteenth century Sen Rikyū (1522–1591) introduced the Tea Ceremony, or *chanoyu*, meaning 'hot water for tea', which was the ceremonial preparation and presentation of *matcha*, powdered green tea. His simple advice was to 'make a delicious bowl of tea; lay the charcoal so that it heats the water; arrange the flowers as they are in the field; in summer suggest coolness; in winter, warmth; do everything ahead of time; prepare for rain; and give to those with whom you find yourself every consideration.' The ceremony elevated tea drinking to an art form; it soon took on important cultural and political significance. The ceremony and its significance is best described by the Irish-Greek writer Patrick Lafcadio Hearn (1850–1904), also known by his Japanese name, Koizumi Yakumo: 'The Tea ceremony requires years of training and practice to graduate in art ... yet the whole of this art, as to its detail, signifies no more than the making and serving of a cup of tea. The supremely important matter is that the act be performed in the most perfect, most polite, most graceful, most charming manner possible.'

2

'Cupan tae' Comes to Europe

Coffee, Chocolate and Coffee Houses

Despite the arrival of tea on the eastern borders of Europe by way of the Ancient Tea-Horse Road, it was some years before tea came to a Europe preoccupied, it seems, with those other beverages, coffee and chocolate.

England's first coffee house was established in Oxford in 1652 at the Angel in the parish of St Peter-in-the-East; Oxford's Queen's Lane Coffee House, opened in 1654, still trades on the corner of Queen's Lane and the High Street. London's first coffee house opened in 1652 in St Michael's Alley, Cornhill. It was run by Pasqua Rosée, an Armenian servant of Daniel Edwards, a trader in Turkish goods for the Levant Company. Coffee houses all over Europe became massively popular for conversation, debate and gossip among tradesmen, politicians, journalists and lawyers. Shares and commodities were bought and sold here – Lloyd's of London grew from Lloyd's coffee house in Abchurch Lane off Lombard Street and the Stock Exchange had its origins in Jonathan's Coffee House. In England alone, by 1675, there were 3,000 or so coffee houses doing business. Pasqua Rosée also set up the first coffee house in Paris in 1672 followed by Procopio Cutò's Café Procope in 1686. It still trades today in the Rue de l'Ancienne Comédie and claims to have been a meeting place for Voltaire, Rousseau, and Diderot. By 1714 tea drinking in Pall Mall was part of the morning routine, according to Daniel Defoe in his *A Tour Through the Whole Island of Great Britain*. In England, coffee houses were also known as 'penny universities' in recognition of their status as the university of life they emulated and the penny admittance fee. Their significance is that the coffee houses also served tea.

Portugal and Holland

Giovanni Batista Ramusio, the traveller and travel writer, wrote about tea in 1559, saying, 'People would gladly give a sack of rhubarb for one ounce of Chai Catai' in his *Delle Navigatione et Viagg*. Rhubarb was highly prized because of its medicinal properties. It was another fifty years or so, though, before tea started to take off in Europe: we have the Dutch and Portuguese to thank for importing tea into Europe from about 1610. Later, the Portuguese shipped their oriental goods to Lisbon, from where Dutch ships transported them to France, Holland, and the Baltic countries. It was not long before the Dutch cut out the Portuguese and the leg to Lisbon, and made inroads into Portuguese trading routes in Asia. At the end of the sixteenth century the Dutch

Peacock Hill coffee estate at Pussellawa, Ceylon – soon to become one of the many tea plantations after the devastating coffee blight. Originally published in O'Brian, *A Series of Fifteen Views in Ceylon*, 1864.

established a trading post at Bantam on Java; the first consignment of tea was shipped from Macau to the Netherlands in 1606 via Bantam in a Dutch East India Company ship in exchange for a cargo of sage. In 1610 the Dutch bought tea from the Japanese on Hirado and shipped it back to the Netherlands. Unrest among the colonists led the emperor to expel all foreigners from Japanese waters for 200 years from 1633; the Portuguese refused to go but the Dutch helped the Japanese to eject them. In return, the Dutch were allowed to stay trading in a restricted commercial capacity. Tea was soon all the rage among the well-heeled Dutch, and spread from the Netherlands to neighbouring countries in continental Western Europe; however, because of its high price it was very much a drink for the wealthy. Every affluent house had its own tea room. The Dutch were the first to add milk to both tea and coffee.

The Dutch East India Company was set up in 1602 to establish trading bases in Indonesia, Japan and other Asian countries. They were granted a monopoly on Dutch trade east of the Cape of Good Hope and west of the Strait of Magellan. By 1637 the company was able to report, 'As tea begins to come into use by some of the people, we expect some jars of Chinese as well as Japanese tea with each ship.' But Chinese xenophobia and protectionism meant that it was not all plain sailing: the Dutch were not received in Canton until 1655. The British were somewhat blind to the commercial potential of tea and only set up a trading post on Formosa (modern Taiwan) in 1672.

Tea Heretics

Between 1635 and 1657 a war raged in the Netherlands in which 'tea heretics' – doctors and academics – argued over the good and bad qualities of tea; the tea-drinking Dutch general public were oblivious, though, to the controversy. Despite the efforts of a Dr

Bontekoe (also known as Dr Cornelius Decker), who recommended the consumption of between fifty and 200 cups a day in his *Diatribe de Febribus* (some believed him to be in the pay of the Dutch East India Company), it was not all good news for tea. A doom-laden Latin treatise, *Commentarius de Abusu Tabaci et Herbae Thee*, written by the German Dr Simon Paulli, warned that tea 'hastens the death of those that drink it, especially if they have passed the age of forty years'. This, though, was the same medical authority who claimed, no doubt from hands-on experience, that 'a girl's breasts rubbed with the juice of hemlock stop growing, but stay properly small and do not change in size'. Another Dutch physician described tea as 'groats and dishwater, a tasteless and revolting beverage!' Nikolas Dirx in his *Observationes Medicae* claimed it was a panacea offering great longevity.

Marie de Rabutin-Chantal, the Marquise de Sevigne, that socialite and letter-writing gossip, found it worthy to note that a friend of hers actually took her tea with milk! But this is the same gossip who declared chocolate to have a defining role in embryology: one of her missives in 1671 tells us that 'the Marquise de Coetlogon took so much chocolate during her pregnancy last year that she produced a small boy as black as the devil, he died'. Soon the 'novelty of the century' had had its day and the Frenchmen resumed their love of wine and coffee. The Germans, after a brief flirtation with tea, returned to their beer. Dutch inns were by now serving tea; guests could order a portable tea set along with a heater, allowing them to make their own tea out in the garden – an early form of the picnic.

(Lady Matchless): 'Ha, ha, ha: love and scandal are the best sweetners of tea.' Henry Fielding, *Love in Several Masques*, 1727

France

Things oriental were very *à la mode*, which was why the powerful Cardinal Jules Mazarin, French Chief Minister from 1641 to 1662, took to tea as an 'Orientalisme Patricienne', hoping that it would also relieve his gout. Louis XIV followed suite in 1665 with the same hopes; he also had it on good authority that the inveterate tea-drinking Japanese and Chinese had low incidences of coronary heart disease.

The health issues surrounding tea were being hotly debated in Paris from as early as 1648. A. M. Morisset described tea as a mental stimulant, but when he presented it to the Faculty of Medicine at the University of Paris, it was rejected and set on fire by adherents of sage.

Not surprisingly, tea was closely associated with the rich and the French aristocracy; when Louis XVI and Marie Antoinette were guillotined during the Revolution in 1793, the fashion for tea was dispatched with them.

Russia

If there were two nations that matched Britain in its obsession with tea then those nations would be Russia and Ireland. Tea (and vodka) has been an inextricable part of Russian culture since the seventeenth century. In 1689, tea was imported from China to Russia by way of a caravan comprising 300 camels on an 11,000-mile round journey which

'The Cultivation of Tea in Assam', published in *The Graphic* in 1875. It shows (from the top left): tea gardens at Cherideo; the teahouse at Mazingah; a bridge in the Vassangor district; women plucking tea at Makepore; tea gardens at Galakee; and the interior of a teahouse.

British tea traders selecting tea in India in the nineteenth century.

HARVEY BROS, & TYLER. LONDON.

lasted sixteen months; furs were given in exchange. The Treaty of Nerchinsk was signed in 1689 – the first treaty between Russia and China, it formalised a common frontier between the two countries, and the opening of the Tea Road caravan route between them. By the 1870s it was reported that 'throughout Russia, particularly in trading towns, not a single man spends a day without drinking tea twice, sometimes three times; and in the countryside those who are better off have come to use the samovar!'

Ireland

Ireland has the honour being the country with the highest *per capita* consumption of tea in the world. On average the Irish person drinks four to six cups every day, or seven pounds of dried tea leaves in a year. Three quarters of the population of 4.5 million are avid tea drinkers. The Irish also have the privilege today of being noted for the consistently high quality of their teas – a happy situation, largely brought about when in 1941 the Irish government established Tea Importers (Eire) Ltd. Their brief was to deal directly with tea producers in the country of origin; no middlemen were permitted to adulterate the relationship between producer and Tea Importers (Eire) Ltd.

Compared with other European countries the cup of tea, or 'cupan tae' in Gaelic, arrived in Ireland comparatively late – probably not before around 1800. Mary Leadbeater's pamphlet published in 1811, *Cottage Dialogues*, suggests that servants were being offered tea morning, noon and night. The concern that the poor would dissipate money on tea also appears in Mary Leadbeater; in her *The Landlord's Friend* of 1813, Lady Seraphina, the land owner, remarks that tea cups are conspicuous by their absence in the kitchen of Winny's cabin. By way of explanation Winny retorts, 'We never were used to tea, and would not choose that our little girl should get a notion of any such thing. The hankering after a drop of tea keeps many poor all their lives.'

The ubiquity of tea paraphernalia in Irish homes is confirmed for us by an article, 'On Tea', in the *Belfast Monthly Magazine* of 31 July 1812: 'In the present age the increase of [tea's] use has been very conspicuous ... even in the obscure hamlet, few are without their tea equipage, which usually forms the most striking object in the cupboard or on the shelf.'

> 'Indeed, madam, your ladyship is very sparing of your tea: I protest, the last I took was no more than water bewitch'd.' Jonathan Swift (1667–1745)

A somewhat alarmist article in the *New York Times* of 8 May 1910 entitled 'Tea is Ireland's Evil – Ranks before Alcohol as an Enemy of Public Health' confirms the ubiquity of tea drinking when it tells that 'the use of tea is now carried to such dangerous excess that it ranks before alcohol as an enemy of the public health ... it is in the poorest parts of the country that the tea evils is most active and hurtful ... the tea is so prepared for use that the liquid, when drunk, has the properties of a slow poison'.

Historically the Irish bought their tea from English auction houses but, during the Second World War, neutral Ireland closed their ports to English shipping, which led to a dramatic reduction in tea imports. The upshot was that Ireland had to find a new source for their tea; that source was through Tea Importers (Eire) Ltd.

Juanita Browne's *Put the Kettle On: The Irish Love Affair with Tea* encapsulates the popular appeal of tea and its fundamental place in Irish society in sixty-five reminiscences from all walks of Irish life down the years. Tea is everywhere in Ireland but Declan Egan was probably referring to a peat bog when he recalled 'The tea on the bog was the best of the lot.'

3

'Chaw' Comes to Britain

Garraway's, Rugg and Samuel Pepys

'Bring me a pot of the best sort of chaw.' These were the words of Richard Wickham in a letter to merchants in Macao: the first known reference to tea by an Englishman, dating from 1615. He ran the British East India Company office in Firando, Japan. In 1625 Samuel Purchas mentions *chia*, in his *Purchas His Pilgrimes*: 'They put as much as a walnut shell may containe, into a dish of Porcelane and drink it with hot water.' Peter Mundy saw it in Fukien in 1637, '*chaa* – only water with a kind of herb boyled in it.' The brewers of London knew all about it; in a pamphlet from 1641 extolling the (dubious) virtues of warm English beer, they quoted an Italian priest who described it as 'the strained liquor of a herb called Chia hot'. In 1659 Daniel Sheldon was anxious to get some for his uncle, Dr Gilbert Sheldon, so that he might 'study the divinity of that herbe, leafe, or whatever else it is'. Money was no object, even 'a viage to Japan or China', if necessary. Daniel's uncle was the Archbishop of Canterbury.

As we have seen, coffee houses began opening in Oxford and London from 1650. Tea was first added to a price list at Thomas Garraway's coffee house in Change Alley, London, in 1657. Garraway had some selling to do to clear his stocks of this mysterious new beverage, so he promoted it through a distribution of pamphlets and an advertisement in *Mercurius Politicus* on 30 September 1658, the first advertisement for a commodity in a London newspaper. His copy read, 'That Excellent, and by all Physicians approved, *China* drink, called by the *Chinese*, *Tcha*, by other nations *Tay alias Tee* ... sold at the Sultaness-head, ye *Cophee-house* in Sweetings-Rents, by the Royal Exchange, *London*.'

Prices were exorbitant: £3 16s per pound. In 1666 a lady made a mail order for brandy and comfits and tea; she paid thirty-one shillings for the brandy and two pounds a pound for the tea. In 1609, Mary, Countess of Argyll, was charged twenty-six pound a pound. The alleged health benefits of tea made an early appearance: tea made the body 'active and lusty ... preserving perfect health until extreme old age ... removeth the obstructions of the Spleen ... very good against the Stone and Gravel, cleaning the Kidneys and Uriters, being drank with Virgins Honey instead of Sugar'. Garraway noted that it was very scarce and 'it hath been only used as Regalia in high Treatments and Entertainments, and Presents made thereof to Princes and Grandees'. The memorial plaque at 32 Cornhill is all that is left of Garraway's; it reads, 'Garraway's Coffee House, a place of great commercial transaction

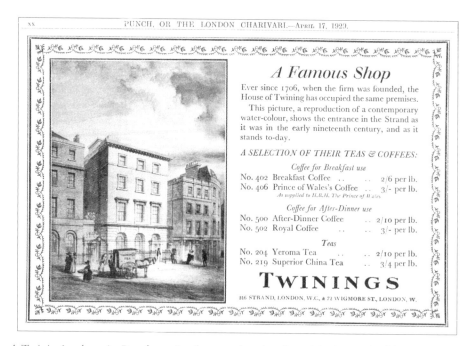

A Twining's advert in *Punch*, 17 April 1929, showing the original 1706 building which still stands and trades to this day at 216 The Strand. There was another branch at 72 Wigmore Street.

and frequented by people of quality.' Other advertisements naturally followed, for example, in the *Tatler* of March 1710, 'The finest Imperial Tea, 18*s*.; Bohee, 12*s*., 16*s*., 20*s*., and 24*s*.; all sorts of Green, the lowest 12*s*. To be had of R. Tate, at the 'Star' in Bedford Court, near Bedford Street, Covent Garden.'

According to the barber Thomas Rugg, writing in his *Diurnal*, 'coffee, chocolate and a kind of drink called *tee*' were 'sold in almost every street in 1659'. The Navy's Clerk of the Acts, Samuel Pepys, ever keen to try anything new, had his first cup of tea on 25 September 1660 while discussing foreign affairs relating to Spain, Holland and France with friends. His diary entry reads, 'I did send for a Cupp of Tee, (a China drink) of which I had never drunk before.' Nearly seven years later, on 28 June 1667, we find Pepys confirming for us the alleged medicinal qualities of tea: 'I went away and by coach home, and there find my wife making of tea, a drink which Mr. Pelling, the Potticary, tells her is good for her cold and defluxions.' If Susanna Centlivre's 1718 play, *A Bold Strike for a Wife*, is anything to go by, Bohea tea was just as popular in Jonathan's coffee house (where the play was set) as coffee.

Catherine of Braganza

Given Portugal's involvement in the early importation of tea to the Netherlands it comes as no surprise that it was a popular drink in affluent Portuguese circles. In 1660 the British East India Company presented the newly crowned Charles II with two pounds two ounces shipped in from Portugal; two years later his queen, Catherine of Braganza, ensured its popularity among the nobility by being seen to be imbibing. Charles himself would take little persuading to join her; he had spent many years in Amsterdam, where tea was readily available. Catherine's tea arrived in chests as part of the dowry sent by her father, King John IV, some of which was ship-loads of luxury goods, some gifts and some to be sold to pay off Charles' debts. The tea qualified as a gift and was enjoyed at and by the English court. Legend has it that when the princess landed at Portsmouth on 13 May 1662 she asked for a calming cup of tea after a somewhat stormy crossing; there was no tea to be had anywhere so she was offered a glass of ale instead. Edmund Waller's poem for the queen's birthday assures her place in the history of tea in Britain:

> Venus her Myrtle, Phoebus has his bays;
> Tea both excels, which she vouchsafes to praise.
> The best of Queens, the best of herbs, we owe
> To that bold nation which the way did show
> To the fair region where the sun doth rise,
> Whose rich productions we so justly prize.
> The Muse's friend, tea does our fancy aid,
> Regress those vapours which the head invade,
> And keep the palace of the soul serene,
> Fit on her birthday to salute the Queen.

'So hear it then ... You cannot make the tea so fast / As I can gulp it down. / I therfore pray thee, Rennie dear, / That thou wilt give to me / With cream and sugar softened well, / Another dish of tea!' Samuel Johnson (1709–1784)

The arrival of tea in Britain was perfectly captured by the American essayist Agnes Repplier in her 1931 essay *To Think of Tea!*: 'Tea had come as a deliverer to a land that called for deliverance; a land of beef and ale, of heavy eating and abundant drunkenness; of grey skies and harsh winds; of strong nerved, stout-purposed, slow-thinking men and women. Above all, a land of sheltered homes and warm firesides – firesides that were waiting – waiting for the bubbling kettle and the fragrant breath of tea.' Repplier is absolutely right: Catherine of Braganza not only made tea *à la mode* in Britain, to some extent she changed the drinking habits of the nation by providing an alternative to stultifying ale or wine. Who knows what effect that had on productivity, decision-making, and behaviour generally? After dinner, women of means started to withdraw from the table and their rumbustious, wine-fuelled, cigar-smoking menfolk to the relative calm of the anteroom and its sewing, conversation, and a nice cup of tea. Although increasing numbers of men imbibed, Henry Savile must have spoken for many when in 1674 he vilified his tea-drinking friends 'who call for tea, instead of pipes and bottles after dinner, a base unworthy Indian practice'. If Charles's queen was a force for tea then so was the British East India Company; their monopoly on Chinese tea ensured an increasingly ready supply and a market in London where eager traders enjoyed high margins. This, and the virtual exclusion of Britain from the Mediterranean and the coffee-exporting Levant during wars with Spain and France, ensured Britain became a nation of tea drinkers while the rest of the continent remained hooked on coffee.

The Honourable British East India Company

Duty of 8*d* per gallon was imposed on liquid tea, as well as on chocolate and sherbet. The British East India Company was a hugely powerful commercial organisation enjoying a monopoly on British trade with the Indies; that is, lands east of the Cape of Good Hope and west of the Straits of Magellan. The only caveat was that it did not meddle with the trade of 'any Christian prince'. Its origins lie in the Royal Charter awarded on 31 December 1600 by Elizabeth I to promote Asian trade. The charter was granted to George, Earl of Cumberland, and 215 knights, and initially bestowed a fifteen-year monopoly. The company name was the Honourable East India Company, or The John Company. The fifteen years turned out to be 250 years. They opened a factory in Bantam, Java, from where they traded in pepper until the factory's closure in 1683. In 1609 James I renewed the charter indefinitely; in 1612, he sent Sir Thomas Roe to visit the Mughal Emperor Nuruddin Salim Jahangir to negotiate a commercial treaty in which the company would have exclusive rights to build factories in Surat and other places. The company would provide the emperor with goods and luxuries from Europe in exchange. By 1647 they owned twenty-three factories in India.

In some ways the company was a law unto itself, enacting bylaws that gave it an economic advantage under a kind of commercial autocracy. It was responsible for the establishment and government of most of the Indian subcontinent, founded Hong Kong and Singapore, triggered the Boston Tea Party, hired Captain Kidd to fight piracy, captured Napoleon and made Elihu Yale rich enough to found ivy league Yale University. The Stars and Stripes is based on its flag, its shipyards provided the template for St Petersburg, New England churches were copies of its London chapel, modern Indian bureaucracy owes everything to it. It gave wool to Japan, chintzes to the USA, spices to the Caribbean, opium to China, porcelain to Russia, polo to Persia – and tea to Britain. By the end of the eighteenth century tea was the company's most lucrative commodity, shipped from Canton to Europe in its fleet of East Indiamen. It maintained its own armies, fleets, navies, currencies, and India; in 1834 when the company was subsumed into the Crown, the 'obituary' in *The Times* noted that 'it accomplished a work such as in the whole history of the human race no other Company ever attempted and, as such, is ever likely to attempt in the years to come'. By 1806 the company owned thirty acres of docks along the Thames estuary.

'Now stir the fire, and close the shutters fast, / Let fall the curtain, wheel the sofa round, / And, while the bubbling and loud-hissing urn / Throws up a steamy column, and the cups / That cheer but not inebriate, wait on each, / So let us welcome peaceful ev'ning in.' William Cowper (1731–1800), *The Task, Book V The Winter Evening*

Charles II was a fan, seduced, no doubt, by the luxurious gifts he received from the company. Charles not only renewed their monopoly but invested in it unprecedented powers, enabling them to use military force to occupy non-Christian places in which they wanted to trade. They could now set up autonomous territorial acquisitions, mint coinage, build fortresses, levy troops and form alliances, make war and peace, and dispense civil and criminal jurisdiction over their territories. Significantly, the port of Bombay came with Catherine's dowry and was handed to the company, for an annual rent of £10 in gold. Bombay was to become the company's Far East trading headquarters, playing a crucial role in the tea trade. In 1664 Macau was opened as a trading post, and to mark the occasion a silver case of tea and cinnamon oil was sent as a gift to Charles and Catherine. In 1700 the company established a permanent base at Canton. The East India Company was the British Crown by proxy.

No wonder then that the company played such a vital and pivotal role in the history of the tea trade in Britain. In 1664 it placed its first order for 100 lbs of China tea to be shipped direct from Java to Britain. Steady importation followed until 1678, when a cargo of 4,713 lbs swamped the market; in 1685 another massive order of 12,070 lbs arrived. As a measure of the company's commercial and political strength, by 1720, 15 per cent of British imports originated in India, most passing through the company; the license was extended until 1766. Tea consumption in Britain exploded: in 1711 it was 142,000 lbs, in 1791 it was 15 million. In money it was worth £12 million between 1789 and 1793; calico was next at £3 million. Tea was worth 6 per cent of Britain's tax revenues.

In 1813, in reaction to growing opposition – not just in the tea industry – the company lost its monopoly of the Indian trade, and in 1834 its China trade monopoly. In 1858, through the Act for the Better Government of India, the Crown took over all of the company's governmental responsibilities, and its 24,000-strong military force was incorporated into the British Army. The company was dissolved on 1 January 1874, through the East India Stock Dividend Redemption Act.

Charles II and the 'Nurseries of Sedition'

The increasing sales of tea in the burgeoning coffee houses had serious economic implications, though, for the Exchequer and for farmers. Farmers saw tea, coffee and brandy as unwelcome competition for their wheat, barley and malt – beer – and wanted them banned. In the 3,000 or so coffee houses operating in 1675 the refreshing cup of tea was often ordered instead of the glass of ale or gin – alcoholic beverages from which the government received substantial tax revenues. Something had to be done to restore the shortfall. In 1672 Charles issued 'A Proclamation to restrain the spreading of false news, and licentious talking of matters of State and Government'. Coffee houses were seen as 'nurseries of sedition' and the public was urged to report any such anti-government scandal-mongering. Nothing much changed, so in 1674 a similar proclamation was published, and another, more punitive still, at the end of 1675: 'A proclamation for the suppression of coffee-houses'. Impossible to police and in the face of public disapproval, the proclamation was rescinded within eleven short days. Coffee houses, unlike the Stuarts, had come to stay. In 1676 the poet Andrew Marvell scorned Charles in his 'Dialogue between Two Horses':

> Though tyrants make laws, which they strictly proclaim,
> To conceal their own faults and to cover their shame ...
> Let the city drink coffee and quietly groan, –
> They who conquered the father won't be slaves to the son.
> For wine and strong drink make tumults increase,

Chocolate, tea, and coffee, are liquors of peace;
No quarrels, or oaths are among those who drink'em
'Tis Bacchus and the brewer swear, *damn'em! And sink'em!*
Then Charles thy edict against coffee recall,
There's ten times more treason in brandy and ale.

Tea Cultivation and Expertise in England

It was an English doctor, James Cunningham, who brought the first living tea plant back to Britain from Chusan in 1702 as documented in his 'Letters to the Publisher from Mr James Cunningham, FRS and Physician to the English at Chusan in China, *Giving an Account of His Voyage Thither, of the Island of Chusan, of the Several Sorts of Tea, of the Fishing, Agriculture of the Chinese, etc. with Several Observations not Hitherto Taken Notice of'*. Further attempts to grow tea plants were made later in the century, first by John Ellis in 1768 with his 'Thea Bihea in Hortus Kewensis', then by the Duke of Northumberland at Syon House around 1771, as referenced in an Act of Parliament; the same Act cites bushes in Kent and in the Physic Garden in Chelsea. We had to wait until 2005 before further attempts were made: these were at the thriving tea plantation at Tregothnan in Cornwall.

In 1848, Samuel Ball wrote the most comprehensive and detailed book on tea ever published, twenty-two years after he retired from his post as East India Company Inspector of Teas, which he held in Canton from 1804 to 1826. As was the tradition, the book's title was a virtual contents list and, as such, gives a clear picture of what the reader could expect to find therein: *An account of the cultivation and manufacture of tea in China: derived from personal observations during an official residence in that country from 1804 to 1826; and illustrated by the best Authorities; Chinese as well as Europeans; with Remarks on the Experiments now making for the introduction of the culture of the Tea Tree in other parts of the world.*

William Melrose was another expert who, aged twenty-five, represented his father's company, Andrew Melrose & Sons of Edinburgh, in Canton from October 1842. Melrose can claim to have shipped the first consignment of tea back to Britain after the end of the East India Company monopoly through Jardine Matheson; the date was 28 November 1833. Other vessels, the *Georgiana*, which arrived in Liverpool in November, and the *Camden*, reaching Glasgow, dispute the claim. Melrose had previously spent time as a tea-broker so was well-qualified to represent his company as an agent: his tea-tasting expertise alone would have repaid handsomely.

Miss Bates: 'No coffee, I thank you, for me – I never take coffee – a little tea if you please.' Jane Austen (1775–1817), *Emma*

Taxing Tea

Until 1689 tax only extended to liquid tea, thus necessitating a whole day for it to be brewed in the morning and barrelled. The man from the revenue, the gauger, would call daily and levy the tax by the barrel on tea actually consumed. Tea was, therefore,

Unloading tea chests
from the *Louden
Castle* in London in
1857. There were
40,000 packages
weighing two million
pounds on board. The
brokers' clerks can
be seen with their top
hats sampling the tea;
they would then call
on the tea merchants.
Originally published in
the *Illustrated London
News*, 1857.

heated up as required throughout the day. Tax was initially 8*d* per gallon, rising steeply
to 16*d* per gallon in 1670; this was twice the tax levied on coffee and indicates that
tea was still considered a luxury beverage. After 1689 tea was taxed in its loose-leaf
form and the five shillings per pound tax was paid on purchase. No doubt this led to
a significant improvement in the taste of the tea, as it could now be brewed fresh on
demand. Compared with the rest of Europe, tea bought in Britain was expensive. The
cheapest in England was the unattractively branded 'Twinings Green Dust' at between
six and twelve shillings per pound; continental tea was the equivalent of five shillings.
In 1706 a small cup of tea at Thomas Twining's Golden Lion tea shop in The Strand
cost one shilling. For the early part of the eighteenth century East India tea duty was
at 14 per cent, with an excise tax of five shillings per pound. In 1745 the excise was
slashed to one shilling, with a significant drop in prices and a significant rise in demand
– consumption leapt from 800,000 lbs in 1745 to 2.5 million in 1750. In 1784, when
duties and tax amounted to 119 per cent, domestic consumption was five million lbs;
the Tea and Window Act reduced duties to 12 per cent and the consumption rocketed to
eleven million lbs in twelve months.

Scotland, through Leith in Edinburgh and the Clyde in Glasgow, and its merchants'
frequent visits to Canton, was as receptive as London to the new beverage; Wales and

Ireland took to tea somewhat later. If Catherine of Braganza was the champion of tea in seventeenth-century England, Mary of Modena, Duchess of York, deserves that accolade in Scotland. She was Catherine's sister-in-law, wife of the Duke of York (later James II of England and James VII of Scotland); she introduced tea at Holyrood Palace in 1680. The royal assent to tea in England continued with the Dutch William and Mary, and Queen Anne, all devotees. Anne was such an avid tea drinker that she exchanged her tiny Chinese teapots for a capacious bell-shaped silver teapot; the earliest tea services date from her reign. Alexander Pope wrote of her in *The Rape of the Lock* in 1711 at Hampton Court (Canto 3, 8–9):

> Here thou, great Anna, whom three realms obey,
> Dost sometimes counsel take and sometimes tea.

Pope shows Hampton Court to be a location for both serious matters of state and more sociable occasions. Pope is using poetic license when he says that she 'sometimes' drank tea; Anne famously drank copious amounts.

Gendering Tea

From the start tea seems to have been associated with women and to have been regarded as a woman's drink. In Richard Ames's satire *The Bacchanalian Sessions: Or the Contention of Liquors*, published in 1693, tea loses out to coffee and other coffee house drinks due to its frivolous nature; Ames describes it as 'a drink much admir'd by the Ladies'. Courtesans were said to prefer it, due probably to its expense and its luxurious image. In 1702 Queen Anne's poet laureate, Nahum Tate, composed his thirty-six-page *Panacea: A Poem upon Tea*, which describes in no small detail the discovery and production of tea – a subject of 'delicacy' and 'decency' perfect as an 'Entertainment for the Ladies'. Duncan Campbell wrote his *A Poem Upon Tea* in 1735, also dedicated to women; here he describes how 'when at Tea they sit' women are 'soberly inclin'd' and 'to one another affable and kind'. Indeed, 'Tea is the School at which they learn their Wit'; the preface asks of 'The Masculine Reader' what he would do 'without some female love and Tea'. Tea, then, represents womanliness and domesticity; the serving of tea in the home was the female equivalent to male socialisation outdoors in the coffee house. 'Tea is indeed the Tobacco of women', said George Poore in 1883.

Selling Tea 'by the Candle'

In 1705 annual importation of tea to England grew to over 800,000 pounds. In 1706 the first of the quarterly auctions for tea was held in Craven House, later known as East India House. These auctions were 'Sold by the Candle', a procedure in which a candle was marked off in inches; it was lit at the start of the bidding and the hammer was brought down when the first inch line was reached, and so on down the candle for each lot. In 1717 the East India Company finally won the right to trade directly with Canton; this increased sales substantially in the 1720s, with average imports around 900,000 pounds per annum rising to 3.7 million pounds in the 1750s. Most of this was green tea, drunk with sugar or preserved lemon. The four main imports were, in order of price, Bohea picked from coarse leaves, Congo, Souchon and Pekoe, the finest. The increasing volumes of imports suggests clearly that the market for tea was increasing dramatically, extending down into the less wealthy man and woman in the street. The 1736 anonymous poem *In Praise of Tea*, also dedicated to the ladies, sums up the socioeconomic situation relating to tea in verse:

> When tea was sold for guineas by the pound,
> The poor a drinking Tea were never found,
> Then only china dishes cou'd be bought
> Burnt in with gold, or else in colours wrought:
> Now tea is cheap, so dishes are the same;
> The pray wherein are they so much to blame.

Thomas Twining typifies the paradox of tea and coffee houses. Twining took over Tom's Coffee House in Devereux Court in 1706 and set about developing his tea business from the shop next door, at the sign of the Golden Lyon, from where he sold tea to other coffee houses, including Button's in Covent Garden. Between 1716 and 1722 Button bought packets of coffee every day, along with other groceries such as Bohea tea, chocolate, sugar, snuff and rum. His coffee cost him between 5s 6d and 6s 8d per pound, while his tea set him back between 16 shillings and 18 shillings per pound. Coffee purchases were four times that of tea but the volume suggests that tea, despite the price, was an increasingly popular choice of beverage in his coffee house. The image of the two drinks, nevertheless, remained quite distinct. Coffee was still a man's drink consumed in the coffee house among like-minded men; women were barred from coffee houses. Tea remained a woman's drink, drunk in the home by women.

'The next opening of the door brought something more welcome; it was for the tea things which Fanny had begun almost to despair of seeing that evening.' Jane Austen (1775–1817), *Mansfield Park*

The Quintessential English Tea Party

The domestication of tea revealed itself in the tea party. Coffee houses sold tea in loose leaf form as a take-away so that it could be brewed at home and enjoyed by women of the wealthier families. It was not a solitary affair though; friends and acquaintances would be invited round to tea parties – the first manifestation of the social aspects of tea drinking beyond the coffee houses. Over time, genteel accoutrements would accompany the occasion to match the genteel company: china tea services, elegant teapots, spoons, silver kettles, jars, tea tables and the like. Servants would set it all up; the hostess would brew and serve. The tea party took place in a special room – the closet, boudoir or private sitting room. An exquisite example survives at Ham House in Richmond. Other citadels of tea converted or built from scratch include Dunham Massey in Cheshire, the Chinese Room at Claydon House in Buckinghamshire modelled on a Chinese teahouse, and Robert Adams' Tea House Bridge at Audley End in Essex. Caddies were kept locked when not in use; it is a measure of the expensiveness of tea that the hostess often carried the key to the caddy around her waist – a precaution against light-fingered staff. Tea was stored in and sipped from Chinese porcelain tea jars and tea bowls, imported from China in the same ships as the tea, where they acted as ballast in the bilges. It is estimated that between 1684 and 1791, 215 million items of porcelain were imported into Europe.

John Wesley, *Tea*-totaller and the 'chambers of death'

One would assume that John Wesley, in his pursuit of temperance, would have been a firm advocate of the social, medical and psychological benefits of tea, particularly as he had a reputation for drinking the stuff while at Charterhouse around 1719, and continued to do so for a further twenty-seven years. Not so. He believed that it caused 'numberless disorders, particularly those of a nervous kind' and was alarmed by 'some Symptoms of a Paralytick disorder', including tremors in the hands, which he and fellow Methodists suffered. In his *Primitive Physick* (which contains over 800 prescriptions for more than 300 different disorders), he clearly states that 'coffee and tea are extremely hurtful to Persons who have weak nerves'. To avoid any doubt, Wesley thundered in 'A Letter to A Friend Concerning Tea' in 1748 that 'when you drink tea it has brought you near the chambers of death'.

Wesley demonised tea in much the same way as he did alcohol; he became a *tea*-totaller in 1746 and recommended that his followers do likewise. He had witnessed similar symptoms to those he had shown at Charterhouse while working among the poor, noting that Londoners' 'nerves [were] all unstrung, bodily Strength quite decayed'. As a good and safe substitute for tea, he recommended 'small' (weak) beer. In 1746, in an address to the London Society, he urged the 100 or so Methodists present to give the money spent on the tea to the needy; tea could be replaced with infusions made from English herbs including sage or mint. Advice was also given on how to refuse politely when offered a cup of tea.

It took his doctor to disabuse Wesley before tea drinking could be resumed by the Methodists, to become a major weapon in the battle for temperance. To celebrate the event, and no doubt to mark his relief at the uplift in sales it would bring, Josiah Wedgwood manufactured a commemorative teapot – at that time the biggest teapot in the world, able to hold a gallon of tea – and presented it to Wesley. Interestingly, the cabinet of John Wesley china in John Wesley's New Room in Bristol includes plates and cups and ... teapots.

'The insipidity of the meeting was exactly such as Elinor had expected ... they quitted it only with the removal of the tea things'. Jane Austen (1775–1817), *Sense and Sensibility*

Tea: Panacea or Pernicious?

Tea parties were a practical solution to the exclusion of tea-loving women from rowdy coffee houses, but they also helped expose a wide-ranging opposition to coffee, tea, drinking chocolate and coffee houses on the grounds of their effect on health and family life. In the Netherlands there was a long-running debate on the medical and social benefits, or otherwise, of beverages such as tea, and some less tolerant aristocrats believed that the lower classes generally should not be permitted to drink tea, arguing that it was the preserve of the wealthy.

One of the first airings of the health debate came with the translation and publication of a volatile French tract, 'Wholesome Advice against the Abuse of Hot Liquors', in 1706. The author, a Dr Duncan from the noted health resort Faculty of Montpelier, argued that while moderate consumption was fine, an excess of hot drinks raised the temperature of blood and internal organs, concluding that 'Excess of Heat is the most Common Cause of Sickness and Death'.

There are many tenuous references to Bible stories and analogies with Greek and Roman mythology; one, for example, claimed that Methuselah never drank hot liquors and lived for nearly a thousand years. Duncan warned that that hot liquors heated up the womb, damaging a woman's fertility; as evidence, he noted it took Rachel, the biblical figure notorious for her hot temper, years to conceive. Before that, Sir Kenelm Digby in his 1669 *Book of Receipts* recommended a wholesome snack after a hard day at the office comprising two egg yolks mixed into a pint of tea. This was guaranteed to 'satisfy all rawness of the stomach' when it 'flew all over the body and into the veins'.

In 1674 women registered their disapproval in a satirical petition against coffee and the family-wrecking coffee houses. Tea, because it was served in these 'Stygian Tap-houses', 'a Pimp to the Tavern', was culpable by association. The petition begins: 'The ... Address of Several Thousands of Buxome Good-Women, Languishing in Extremity of Want' and goes on to expatiate on the numerous effects coffee and the coffee houses have on family and married life:

For the continual flipping of this pitiful drink is enough to *bewitch* Men of two and twenty, and tie up the *Codpiece-points* without a Charm. It renders them that use it as *Lean* as Famine, as Rivvel'd as *Envy*, or an old meager Hagg over-ridden by an Incubus. They come from it with nothing *moist* but their snotty Noses, nothing *stiffe* but their Joints, nor *standing* but their Ears ... Men by frequenting these *Stygian Tap-houses* will usurp on our Prerogative of *tattling*, and soon learn to exceed us in *Talkativeness* ... that our Husbands may give us some other *Testimonial* of their being Men, besides their *Beards* and wearing of empty *Pantaloons*: That they no more run the hazard of being *Cuckol'd* by *Dildo's*: But returning to the good old strengthening Liquors of our Forefathers; that Natures *Exchequer* may once again be replenisht, and a Race of Lusty Hero's begot.

In 1699 John Ovington, chaplain to William III, advised Queen Mary that tea was quite the panacea. It 'cures everything under the sun, from gravel [to] vertigo and corrects nauseous humours that offend the stomach, throwing off abundances of those crudities created in the body through excess'. Possibly of more personal interest to Mary, he goes on to say that [tea] 'reconciles men to sobriety, and may be deemed an anti-Circe, counter charming the enchanted cup, and changing the beast into man'.

In 1826, a London tea dealer (obviously biased) published a book contesting the claims that tea drinking brought on 'nervous disorders', cogently arguing instead that irregular exercise, the absence of a healthy diet and lack of sleep may be the causes. He added that tea 'quenches the most burning thirst, and cheers the spirits without heating the blood ... I am inclined to believe that the man who could willingly forgo the pleasures of the tea-table and society around it, wants that kind of congenial spirit without which life would be a burden, and the world a dreary waste'. He reminded his readers that the government dispensed a tea ration to the Navy, unconcerned lest 'our future enemies will have to contend with bilious and nervous sailors, instead of hearts of oak, and sinews of iron'.

In 1730 Thomas Short, a Scottish doctor, set about destroying as groundless the 'Japanick observations' claimed by Ten Rhijn. But Short's arguments were balanced and experiential; his conclusions were analytical; he even appreciated the economic benefits of the trade. Short, in fact, paved the way for the empirical scientific and medical studies of food and nutrition that were to proliferate in the twentieth century. Short correctly observed that green tea was effective against migraine.

The distinguished Quaker John Coakley Lettsom wrote his MD thesis at Leiden University in 1769, *The Natural History of the Tea Tree*. In 1773 he founded the prestigious Medical Association of London, which survives today as the oldest medical society in the United Kingdom. When he inherited his father's sugar plantations in the British Virgin Islands, the first thing he did was free the slaves. His opposition to tea was a selfless act performed in full knowledge that any reduction in consumption would have impacted on his sugar business – tea was routinely sweetened with sugar. Lettsom experimented with tea, injecting the stomachs of frogs and dogs with green and black tea of differing strengths; paralysis occurred in the frogs injected with the black tea, but not the green. To Samuel Johnson he was one of the doctors who 'extend the art of torture'. Experiments with beef showed that when immersed in weak tea it turned putrid, thus leading to the correct conclusion that tea is an antiseptic. Lettsom believed that tea had good and bad points; in the healthy person it was fine, in the infirm it caused them to be 'fluttered', in the anxious and nervous it caused trembling in the hands. A tea broker called Marsh ingested a good deal of tea dust and suffered from 'giddiness, headache, universal spasms, and loss of speech and memory' – cause of death was 'effluvia of tea'. In a similar case the patient was bled and electric-shocked but to no avail; Lettsom conceded that it may have been the shocks that killed him.

'Sir John never came to the Dashwoods without either inviting them to dine at the Park the next day, or to drink tea with them that evening.' Jane Austen (1775–1817), *Northanger Abbey*

The truth of it all clearly lay somewhere between the pernicious and the panacea. The curmudgeonly William Cobbett did not approve; he wrote in his *Cottage Economy*, published in 1822, that 'it is notorious that tea has no useful strength in it; and that it contains nothing nutritious; that it, besides being good for nothing, has badness in it, because it is well-known to produce want of sleep in many cases, and in all cases, to shake and weaken the nerves'. He calculated precisely how much the working classes could save if they drank beer instead. In conclusion, tea was a harbinger of social disaster and doom. He ranted, 'I view tea drinking as a destroyer of health, an enfeebler of the frame, an engenderer of effeminacy and laziness, a debaucher of youth and a maker of misery for old age.' What could be worse? Not beer. Beer is much cheaper than tea, suitable for all except the youngest child. Five quarts (just over a pint) a day should be enough for everyone except drunkards. Tea, on the other hand, is a weak form of laudanum, a complete waste of time and money. Tea kills pigs: 'Give him the fifteen bushels of malt and he will repay you in ten score of bacon or thereabouts. But give him the 730 tea messes, or rather begin to give them to him, and give him nothing else, and he is dead from hunger, and bequeaths you his skeleton, at the end of about seven days ... tea drinking has done a great deal in bringing this nation into the state of misery in which it now is.' Tea leads men and boys to idleness; it encourages 'a softness, an effeminacy, a seeking for the fireside, a lurking in the bed, and in short, all the characteristics of idleness'. Tea leads girls to prostitution; it 'does little less for the girls, to whom the gossip of the tea-table is no bad preparatory school for the brothel'.

The argument raged on into the late nineteenth century. In 1876 W. B. Tegetmeier (1816–1912), the English naturalist, friend of Charles Darwin, writer and journalist on domestic science, declared in his *Manual of Domestic Economy* that tea 'pleasantly excites the nervous system, increases respiration, and the action of the skin, and tends to quicken digestion. It has a decidedly soothing effect upon the action of the heart, and hence is often advantageously employed in cases of palpitation and headache.' Among other polemics there was a nothing if not blunt article by Dr J. E. Cooney in the *Windsor Magazine*, entitled *The Dangers of Tea Drinking* and syndicated to the *San Francisco Call*, 27 October 1895, and the New York *London Queen*, 10 November 1895. The 'pernicious habit of tea-drinking' is described thus:

> the evil effects of tannin in tea, are readily seen by its ravages on the throats and stomachs of tea tasters. Dyspepsia ... is often caused and increased by tea drinking. In flatulent dyspepsia few substances are more to be avoided than tea ... women – are the chief sufferers from this most distressing and unpleasant variety of indigestion – being great tea drinkers ... The mental depression is often distressing, varying in degree from slight dejection ... to the extremes of melancholia or suicidal monomania.

But by then it was all over; tea was here to stay, like it or not – and most people liked it. The first National Food Inquiry in 1863 found that 'the use of tea may now be said to be universal', and in 1878 Samuel Phillips Day confirmed in his *Tea: Its Mystery and History* that 'what was first regarded as a luxury, has now become, if not an absolute necessity, at least one of our accustomed daily wants, the loss of which would cause more suffering and excite more regret than would the deprivation of many things which once were counted as necessities of life'.

The Duke of Wellington liked to drink tea from a Wedgwood teapot during his battles, because it kept his head clear; what could be more British? What part could be more crucial for tea to play in British history? C. H. Denyer, in an article entitled 'The Consumption of Tea and Other Staple Drinks' published in *The Economic Journal* in 1983, concurred: 'We are now almost justified in calling tea the English national drink; the more so as we take of it as much as all the rest of Europe put together.'

'Tea' and 'British' were now synonymous; Tea and Britain were officially one. George Gissing had summed it up when he said, 'Nowhere is the English genius of domesticity more notably evident than in the festival of afternoon tea. The mere chink of cups and saucers turns the mind to happy repose.'

The Jonas Hanway: Dr Johnson Tea Wars

In 1756 the philanthropist, seasoned traveller and London merchant Jonas Hanway was an implacable opponent of tea drinking. He was also the first man to sport an umbrella – much to the derision of his fellow pedestrians. Hanway was determined to rid Britain of tea, and was happy to die in the attempt. He reported in his *An Essay on Tea* that tea was '... pernicious to health, obstructing industry and impoverishing the nation' because tea drinking had led to a depletion of the workforce to the detriment of agricultural and manufacturing output. He added that the country was now vulnerable to enemy attack because the pool of fit and able recruits was diminished: 'What an army has gin and tea destroyed.' Ending the tea trade would allow the Navy to build a seventy-four-gun battle ship with the money saved. Hanway estimated that tea was costing the Treasury £2,691,665 per year; £3,041,666 if labour costs are included. He computed that the cost in lost tax revenues incurred by ending the trade in tea would be £300,000 per year, but that could be compensated for by raising sumptuary taxes on coaches, gold and silver, women's jewellery, servants, periwigs and playing cards. He goes on to ask of women,

> How many sweet creatures of your sex languish with a weak digestion, low spirits, lassitudes, melancholy, and twenty disorders, which, in spite of the faculty, have yet no names, except the general one of nervous complaints? Let them ... leave off drinking tea, it is more than probable, the greatest part of them will be restored to health.

Tea, moreover, will 'convulse the bowels' and causes bad teeth, particularly among the ladies. Hanway insinuated that tea drinking among women made them ugly; 'There is not quite so much beauty in this land as there was.' He asserted that the children of poor mothers were dying because their mothers were spending their money on tea; 'Those will have tea who have not bread.' As evidence he cited an experiment in which a pig's tail was immersed in water and heated to forty-six degrees – the same temperature at which tea is drunk. The porcine skin peeled off, *ergo* the same thing was happening inside the human stomach. If further proof were needed, 'You have seen how the hands of a washerwoman are shrivelled by hot water.' He concludes: 'If doctors spend too long debating its effects ... the patient will be dead before the consultation breaks up.' Tea drinking led to suicide and the death of breast-fed babies: 'The poor infant left neglected expires while she is sipping her tea.'

Dr Samuel Johnson rallied to tea's help, lampooning Hanway in a review published in *The Literary Magazine* in 1757 and declaring himself an incorrigible aficionado, 'a hardened and shameless tea-drinker, who has, for twenty years, diluted his meals with only the infusion of this fascinating plant; whose kettle has scarcely time to cool; who with tea amuses the evening, with tea solaces the midnight, and, with tea, welcomes the morning'. But for Johnson, 'tea's proper use is to amuse the idle, and relax the studious, and dilute the full meals of those who cannot use exercise, and will not use abstinence'. His reputation preceded him: Boswell said, 'I suppose no person ever enjoyed with more relish the infusion of that fragrant leaf than Johnson,' while John Northcote chimed, 'Johnson's extraordinary, or rather extravagant, fondness for tea did not fail to excite notice wherever he went.'

The clamour for social engineering for the feckless and feminine was taken up again in 1758 when the anonymous, vitriolic pamphlet *The Good and Bad Effects of Tea*

Consider'd was circulated. It argued that tea drinking was fit only for the middle and upper classes, and it should be kept from 'persons of an inferior rank and mean abilities'. Afternoon tea drinking among working-class women meant that they were 'neglecting their spinning knitting etc spending what their husbands are labouring hard for, their children are in rags, gnawing a brown crust, while these gossips are canvassing over the affairs of the whole town, making free with the good name and reputation of their superiors'.

'Thank God for tea! What would the world do without tea? How did it exist? I am glad I was not born before tea. I can drink any quantity when I have not tasted wine; otherwise I am haunted by blue-devils by day, and dragons by night.' Sydney Smith (1771–1845), quoted in *A Memoir of the Reverend Sydney Smith: Volume I* by his daughter Lady Saba Holland (1855)

Duty-Free Tea and the Smugglers

The concerns of Hanway and others of like mind regarding the dissolute poor were initially largely unfounded. One pound of tea in 1700 still cost the average skilled worker about three weeks' wages; tea was still very much a rich man and woman's beverage. The need to fund the war against Spain saw the price of tea rise to an extortionate five shillings per pound; smuggled tea increased. In 1745, however, duty on tea was slashed from four shillings to one shilling by Henry Pelham, bringing the price within the reach of more people; illicit tea decreased. This only lasted five years, though; a new increase saw smuggling rise again. In 1778 twenty tons of tea were landed at Trerea in Cornwall from just one boat. Between 1822 and 1824, the House of Commons reported that 19,000 lbs of tea were seized. And it was by no means just the usual suspects who were at it. The diary entries of a Revd James Woodforde reveal that this man of the cloth was up to his dog collar in it and seemed to see no wrong in it. Henry Shore's *Smuggling Days and Smuggling Ways*, published around 1835, elucidates the ways in which tea was smuggled in: in cases fitted between the ships' timbers or on the person concealed beneath capes, under petticoat trousers or tarpaulin jackets.

A big change came in 1784 when William Pitt the Younger, acting on advice from tea dealer Richard Twining, brought in his Commutation Act: it reduced the duty on tea from 119 per cent to a mere 12.5 per cent. This change was reflected in the staggering increase in imports brought in by the East India Company: £14,000 in 1700, £969,000 in 1760, and £1,777,000 in 1790. The reduction in duty, though, was not intended as an act of philanthropy or a plan to impoverish the Exchequer; it was implemented as a strategy in the war against tea smuggling, as tea had joined hard liquor, tobacco and other commodities as a target for the ubiquitous smuggler.

It is estimated that 7 million pounds in weight of tea, also known as 'dry goods', was lost to the Treasury during the eighteenth century; this compares with the 5 million pounds landed legally. The black economy was an everyday fact of life for up to 50,000 people in England alone, and left a hole estimated to be equivalent to one quarter of England's foreign trade. Jonas Hanway, perhaps with an axe to grind, claimed he saw forty tea runners in Douglas harbour on the Isle of Man; moreover, the owner of the island, the Earl of Derby, was allegedly taking one shilling for every pound weight of contraband tea landed. Nationwide, more than 200 ships were known to be involved in smuggling. To some extent the government only had itself to blame; they stood by while the monopolistic East India Company kept prices high to protect their margins. Quite inadvertently, the company had assisted smuggling by allowing officers to conduct private trade on board their ships. Many took the opportunity to profit by selling tea to smugglers. Most tea was smuggled in from Europe and shipped into Britain via the Channel Islands and the Isle of Man. At first it was largely small scale, with small boats carrying no more than sixty chests per journey; tea was then sold on to local shopkeepers.

Tea smuggling was by no means confined to the south and the Isle of Man. In the north-east, too, it was the staple commodity for the smuggler for most of the eighteenth century. It is believed that most if not all the inhabitants of Saltburn, Staithes, Runswick Bay and Robin Hood's Bay were involved in the illicit trade, and Whitby was not exempt. An intricate and extensive network of caves, tunnels and concealed cupboards kept the contraband underground and hidden in all of these locations. The skippers of the ships and boats earned £250 a run, the sailors and overland porters £5 and the labourers and armed lookouts on the beach one guinea.

The combination of the East India Company's monopolistic price fixing and the high rate of duty made tea very profitable for the smuggler. The high value to weight ratio, ease of transportation and the margins obtained on the Dutch tea market on a 6d to 1s per pound purchase selling for 4s to 10s per pound made it the ideal commodity. Even after Pitt had torpedoed the market when he reduced the duty, tea was put to good use as ballast by the smugglers. Leaves masquerading as tea, coloured with rosemary and other adulterations, pushed margins even higher.

Smuggling operations grew considerably bigger in the 1760s when the absence of expensive wars led to increased trade with China. To Scottish excise officers this was the 'new mode' of smuggling: violent gangs crewed large, heavily armed ships, capable of transporting hundreds of chests of tea and gallons of spirits alike. Smuggled tea was now penetrating far inland, reflecting the legal distribution to the extent that smugglers' ships could even be insured against loss or seizure at Lloyd's of London.

Depressed tax revenues were not the only economic consequence of smuggling. In the 1780s an anonymous pamphleteer bemoaned that thousands of labourers had deserted the fields for the more lucrative business of smuggling: 'Thousands … who would otherwise be employed in fishing, agriculture etc, to the emolument of this kingdom are now supported in drunkenness, rioting, and debauchery by their iniquitous traffic; – a traffic obviously productive of so numerous a train of evils, that prudence, common honesty, decency, order, and civil government, unitedly cry out for redress.'

Smuggling obviously had a significant impact on the profits of the East India Company. Richard Twining observed in his *Observations on the Tea & Window Act and on the Tea Trade* of 1784 that contraband tea was the East India Company's biggest rival, indeed they shared the trade equally between them. This was partly responsible for the company's decision to offload surplus tea on the American market, ultimately leading to the Boston Tea Party and the American War of Independence. The price of tea had to come down dramatically to stifle smuggling, and the East India Company lobbied for the duty to be lowered. As we have seen, Pitt did his worst but the situation only lasted a few years before wars with France necessitated a rise in duty, which saw it peak at 96 per cent. The smugglers were back in business. England's coastline was left exposed – not just to the French but to the smugglers too – many vessels had been requisitioned by the Royal Navy, and many of the dragoons who reinforced the revenue men had left to fight the French. Ports such as Copenhagen, Calais, Dunkirk, Flushing and Ostend could supply tea at less than one-sixth of the official duty paid price in Britain. Letters of credit were even accepted as payment in addition to cash, and access to French ports was permitted to smugglers even during the Napoleonic Wars.

'Surely everyone is aware of the divine pleasures which attend a wintry fireside: candles at four o'clock, warm hearthrugs, tea, a fair tea-maker, shutters closed ... tea will always be the favoured beverage of the intellectual.' Thomas de Quincy (1785–1859), *Confessions of an English Opium Eater*

The Adulterators and Second-Hand Tea

Smuggling was not the only illicit trade surrounding tea. Adulteration was an easy way of maximising profits and so became common practice. From the beginning, tea imported into Britain was prey to adulteration; an Act of 1730 cited *terra japonica* being routinely used to dye tea previously diluted with other leaves, or 'second-hand' tea – tea that had already been used. Thomas Short in his 1730 *A Dissertation Upon Tea* and John Lettsom in his *Natural History of the Tea Tree* of 1772 allege that the Chinese often adulterated tea well before it reached Britain. The traveler Robert Fortune witnessed it first-hand and described it in his 1852 *A Journey to the Tea Countries of China*. So the precedent was set, and the bootleggers did not take long to see that the cost of tea could be reduced considerably by selling tea leaves that had already been used or adulterated somehow. 'Lie tea' has been defined as 'the dust of the tea leaves – sometimes of other leaves – and sand, made up by means of starch into little masses, which are afterwards painted so as to resemble either black or green Gunpowder'. Chemically enhanced tea was bogus leaves boiled with ferrous sulphate and coloured with a palette of Prussian blue, verdigris, tannin, or black carbon before resale. Molasses, clay, sulphate of lime or gypsum were also used to bulk up tea and masquerade the fraud. 'Smouch' was particularly noxious: this comprised ash tree leaves dried and soaked in sheep dung then mixed with a sprinkling of real tea. Dry sloe, elder, hawthorn and liquorice leaves mixed with expended tea was another favourite. Some 'teas' sold contained no tea at all, made instead from the dried leaves of other plants. *The Family Herald* put it well in a feature on Fortune's book: 'We Englishmen swallow tea, go to bed, turn and toss ... complain of unstrung nerves and weak digestion, and visit the doctor, who shakes his head and says, "tea!" ... but what he means is metallic paint.'

In 1756 Jonas Hanway described how maids were making a bit on the side by drying and then selling off used leaves: 'The industrious nymph who is bent on gain may get a shilling a pound for such tea. These leaves are dyed in solution of Japan earth.' Falsification of tea continued to be a major problem in the nineteenth century. In 1817, one tea dealer described the public paranoia surrounding adulterated tea 'almost as a secret assassin, ready to enter every man's house to poison him and his family. It almost converted the English into a nation of botanists.' In 1844 Robert Warington, in a report for the Chemical Society, concluded 'that all the green teas that are imported into this country are faced, or covered superficially with a powder consisting of either Prussian blue and sulphate of lime or gypsum ... with occasionally a yellow or orange-coloured vegetable substance'. The first national food survey in 1863 looked at the food of the poorer classes, and it found that 'tea was by now a necessity, 99 per cent of all the families consuming it at the average rate of ½ oz. per adult weekly, 2¼ oz. per family'. The working classes were especially prone to being sold adulterated teas.

There was a moral dimension to the issue too. In 1818 Sir John Sinclair extolled the virtues of tea and of teatime in his *The Code of Health and Longevity*. To him tea was 'a valuable addition ... to solid food ... correcting the pernicious qualities which some waters possess'. It lifted the spirits, aided digestion and was effective against stones; it increased sobriety. Teatime he describes as

> the pleasing occupation which the tea-table furnishes, the beauty of the manufacture in which this preparation of *liquid cookery* is carried on and circulated, the cheerfulness and lightness of the meal, compared with the solemnity and business-like appearance of a substantial dinner all tend to make *tea* a favourite beverage. *Tea time* indeed, is perhaps the most pleasant period of the day, in domestic life. Tea may be regarded, as having been, at least one means of expelling the remains of drunken barbarism from among our countrymen.

> 'The liquid doctors rail at, and that I will quaff in spite of them, and when I die we'll toss up which died first of drinking tea.
>
> 'Though we eat little flesh and drink no wine, Yet let's be merry; we'll have tea and toast; custards for supper, and an endless host of syllabubs and jellies and mincepies, and other such ladylike luxuries.' Percy Bysshe Shelley (1792–1822)

To adulterate tea was, in short, to wreck all of this. Purity, integrity and a whole way of life were compromised. Critically, it was English (British?) purity and integrity, and the English way of life which were being undermined. By now, tea drinking was being recognised as something peculiarly English, and, as in times past, womanly. The definition of 'tea' in the 1879 edition of *Cassell's Dictionary* runs as follows: 'The use of this beverage amongst English people, and especially amongst English women, has increased in the most extraordinary manner, so that it has been said that if to be an Englishman is to eat beef, to be an English woman is to drink tea.'

The moral issue was argued time and time again throughout the century, for example in Dr George Sigmond's *Tea; Its Effects, Medicinal and Moral* (1839), Leitch Ritchie's *The Social Influence of Tea* (1848), Gideon Nye's *Tea and the Tea Trade* (1850), Samuel Philips Day's *Tea: Its Mystery and History* (1878), Dr Gordon Stables' *Tea: the Drink of Pleasure and Health* (1883), and Arthur Reade's *Tea and Tea Drinking* (1884).

One of the impacts of widespread adulteration was a swing towards black tea in the market, partly to avoid consumption of those often toxic colourants. Adding milk to tea also became popular. Both smuggling and adulteration then, illegal and dangerous as they were, had an enduring influence on of tea consumption in Britain. Thanks to the smugglers, tea, and *ersatz* tea, could be obtained relatively cheaply; the smugglers' distribution networks allowed tea to spread into the countryside and the towns and cities inland from the coasts. False tea was cheap. All of this served to swell the market to include ordinary people as well as the wealthy.

The expanding market did not go unnoticed. The Duc de la Rochefoucauld remarked in his *A Frenchman in England* in 1784 that 'throughout the whole of England the drinking of tea is general ... though the expense is considerable, the humblest peasant has his tea twice a day like the rich man'. Rochefoucauld probably was not aware that that 'humblest peasant' was getting his tea duty free from the smugglers. In 1797 Sir Frederick Morton Eden, writer on poverty and groundbreaking social investigator, observed the ubiquity of tea among the poor. In his *The State of the Poor* he notes that 'any person who will give himself the trouble of stepping into the cottages of Middlesex and Surrey at meal-times, will find that, in poor families, tea is not only the usual beverage in the morning and evening, but is generally drunk in large quantities at dinner'.

With a certain amount of righteous indignation, tea traders demanded that the government start inspecting tea to prevent *ersatz* versions entering the country. John Horniman, who had been selling his tea in labelled packets from 1826, successfully availed himself of the branding and marketing opportunities this gave him and emblazoned his labels with descriptions of the tea inside as 'wholesome' and 'pure'. Later, when tea was being imported from British India and Ceylon, it was marketed as 'British' tea, ergo good, pure tea. This may have done something to stem the flow of bogus tea that was imported, but it conveniently overlooked the domestic falsification that continued apace – in the 1840s there were probably eight factories in London alone involved in adulteration. Indeed, in 1851 Henry Mayhew exposed the rampant and illicit trade in a series of articles for the *Morning Chronicle* published as 'London Labour and the London Poor'. The 1875 Customs Act required that all imported tea be subject to inspection, thus effectively ending Chinese adulteration, but not British. It would have come as little consolation to tea manufacturers and traders that chocolate and cocoa were similarly blighted. The purity issue was to become a key factor in the manufacturing and advertising of tea.

Tea, Temperance and Tea Rooms

We have seen how John Wesley vacillated over the rights and wrongs of tea drinking. The eighteenth century saw a massive increase in the consumption of spirits, mainly gin, rising from half a million gallons in 1684 to 5½ million in 1735. Excessive drinking continued apace in England in the nineteenth century, particularly among the less well off, not least because alcohol was the only really safe and easily obtainable means of quenching thirst. Water was often contaminated and tea and coffee were expensive, cocoa prohibitively so and still hard to come by.

The Temperance Society, founded in the 1820s, encouraged people to sign a pledge to give up alcohol, and millions did so with good intentions. This usually took place at mass meetings at which tea would be served. The Quakers and Methodists, both leading supporters of the Temperance Movement, also served tea at their meetings. There arose a general need to have a congenial place in which to drink tea, swapping the drink-fuelled discussion in the public house for an environment which promised something a little more sober. This led to the opening of temperance bars, and a revival of the coffee house. The new coffee house, though, was very different from its seventeenth-century ancestor: it was no longer exclusive to the wealthy (gentle)men, who had now taken refuge in the cocoa houses and the gentlemen's clubs that grew out of them. The new patrons were ordinary people, men *and* women. By the 1880s tea rooms and tea shops became popular and fashionable, especially among women. Women now had a respectable place in which they could meet, chat and relax with dignity – and in comfort and safety, with no defamatory questions regarding their morality. Twining's Golden Lyon had led the way in 1706; it was a more salubrious place than the average coffee shop. Apothecaries, grocers and coffee shops were joined in the tea-rush by jewellers, goldsmiths, mercers, milliners and glassware shops: if well-heeled ladies were the clientele then tea was a profitable sideline.

Tea drinking was essential to the temperance meeting and was sometimes something of a logistical challenge. In Preston 1,200 attended the society Christmas meeting in 1833 and were all served a cup of tea. A 200-gallon boiler was pressed into service, and the waiters were 'reformed drunkards' according to Arthur Reade in *Tea and Tea Drinking*. William Carter in his *The Power of God* of 1865 describes seventy different recent tea events comprising between four and five hundred attendees. Tea with a cause caught on: the Anti-Corn Law League served it at their meetings, as did the Vegetarian Society.

Some enlightened employers had the sense and vision to realise the benefits of tea over alcohol and how the encouragement of the former over the latter would be in the interest both of the workers (health) and the management (productivity). In 1878 the landowner T. Bland Garland stopped supplying beer and gave them a hefty pay increase and a limitless supply of tea. He bought a boiler and built a fireplace in the field, arranging for local women to prepare fresh tea for the labourers from dawn to dusk. One advocate was Sir Philip Rose (b. 1816), who observed that farm workers 'were in better condition at the conclusion of the day, less stupid and sullen', with no sign of hangovers the next morning. Flora Thompson, too, notices how the pack-up for the labourer in the fields included 'tin bottles of cold tea'. During the First World War the Ministry of Munitions Health Committee endorsed the tea break – as did Ernest Bevin in 1940 – in the morning, in the afternoon and, crucially, at the end of the working day.

'Crammed as they on earth were crammed, some sipping punch, some sipping tea, / But as you by their faces see, all silent and all damned.' Percy Bysshe Shelley (1792–1822), from Peter Bell's hell

The London Tea Auction, 1679–1998
We have seen how tea was sold 'by the candle' at the quarterly auctions which took place in the magnificent East India House. Contemporary reports attest to the rowdiness a tea auction generated – this one is from an anonymous tea dealer in 1826: 'To the uninitiated

a Tea sale appears to be a mere arena in which the comparative strength of the lungs of a portion of his Majesty's subjects are to be tried. No one could for an instant suspect the real nature of the business for which the assemblage was congregated.'

Everything changed in April 1834 when the East India Company lost its monopoly and tea became a 'free trade' commodity. The tea auction moved to a dowdy dance studio, then to the newly built London Commercial Salerooms in Mincing Lane. Tea merchants followed the auction and set up offices in Mincing Lane, the 'Street of Tea'. Auctions now were held monthly, and then weekly, reflecting the upsurge in popularity of tea; selling 'by the candle' was replaced. Tea could now be landed in Liverpool, Leith, Glasgow and Bristol as well as in London. To take advantage of the ending of the monopoly, tea dealers such as Henry Tuke & Co. of York opened an office in Liverpool with warehousing in Bristol and Hull. These shrewd moves streamlined importation and enabled them to sell and transport more economically, direct from different parts of the country. Hitherto, all the tea had come laboriously by sea or road from east London, sometimes with on-shipment as far as Edinburgh.

Tea was pouring in from India, China, Ceylon and East Africa for auction. Such was the influx that particular days of the week were devoted to the sale of teas from individual countries. Despite the best efforts of the Luftwaffe during the London Blitz, one-third of all the world's tea was still bought in Mincing Lane in the mid-1950s. Only the two world wars interrupted the London Tea Auction – the auctions lasted until 29 June 1998, when email took over. The auction had been dealt a blow after India (1947), Sri Lanka

George Cruickshank (1792–1878) always had his finger on the political and social pulse of Britain. This 1848 cartoon is titled *A Good Cup of Tea (When the Duty is Taken Off)* – a reference to the relaxation of the high duty on tea at the time and the resulting popularity with all classes. Note the size of the urn and the capacious cups the ladies drink from. First published in George Cruikshank's *Four Hundred Humorous Illustrations*, Simpkin, Marshall, Hamilton, Kent & Co.

(1948) and Kenya (1963) gained independence. Naturally, tea estate owners now elected to sell their teas locally rather than going through the time and expense of shipping them to London for auction. Local auctions were accordingly set up in Calcutta, Colombo and Mombassa. Methods of international trading were changing as well: telephone, email and the Internet largely obviated the need for a physical auction house.

'[Alice Wilson] ventured to ask [Mary] if she would come in and take tea with her that very evening ... she borrowed a cup ... half an ounce of tea and quarter of a pound of butter went far to absorb her morning wages.' Elizabeth Gaskell (1810–1865), *Mary Barton*

Tea Clippers

The termination of the East India Company's contract to import tea from China on an exclusive basis had serious ramifications for the supply of tea to Britain and brought about significant changes. The monopoly had meant that speed was never of the essence, rather, it was in the interest of the company to protect margins and maximise profits. The more tea they could transport in one ship the better – no matter how long it took to deliver. The work horses of the East India fleet were the cumbersome East Indiaman ships, which could carry a massive 1,200 tons of cargo. A typical round trip took nearly two years, with the East Indiamen sailing from Britain in January and arriving in China in September via the Cape of Good Hope. Having loaded, they would usually reach Britain again in the following September. Hence the saying, 'A slow boat to China.'

When the East India Company lost its monopoly in 1834 speed suddenly became an issue for the first time in the tea trade: tea was now traded freely. It did not take long for a number of sailors to realise that the first vessels to arrive in Britain with their cargoes of tea would reap the best rewards. Not only did it allow open access to a market avid for tea but it satisfied a popular demand for the freshest tea possible – the earlier the arrival, the fresher the tea. The prize was the 'First Chop', harvested in April and May. How then to expedite this precious cargo? The slow, old 500-ton East Indiamen were patently not the long-term answer; something much, much quicker was required.

The answer lay with the Americans, who built the first clippers, modelled on the swift and streamlined Baltimore clipper, with up to thirty-five sails, six to a mast. They were called clippers either because they 'clipped off' the miles or because one of the meanings of 'to clip' was to run or fly swiftly. We still use the phrase 'to go at a fair clip'. Decisive action was needed if British merchants were to join this new age in maritime trade. The *Stornoway* was the first British clipper to be built, in Aberdeen in 1850, and in 1851 British ship owner Richard Green built the *Challenger*; his aim was to out-sail the Americans. Loaded with tea, the *Challenger* left Canton in 1852, with 'the most valuable cargo of tea and silk ever to be laden in one bottom'. She was to come up against the American *Challenge*, famous for her speed. Bets were laid on the winner: *Challenger* arrived in London two days before the *Challenge*.

The opening of the Suez Canal in November 1869 put an end to the exciting and majestic clipper races. The decidedly unromantic steam ships were now more economical tea transporters, and chugging their way through the canal, they replaced the elegant clippers.

The Sun Sets on the East India Company

Tea companies, not least Twinings, had long lobbied for the termination of the East India Company monopoly. American independence in 1783 brought with it the loss of a big market in the west as the Americans plied their own trade with China – this also raised questions about the trade monopolies in the East. India went first in 1813 but China remained; China was still synonymous with tea.

When renewal of the 1600 charter came up in 1833, there was much opposition among traders bemoaning the restrictive practices of the company: fixing tea prices artificially high and restricting the supply of tea to increase global prices. The level of antipathy can be gauged by this anonymous pamphlet from 1824: 'The lordly grocers of Leadenhall Street [the then base of the company] have most scandalously abused the monopoly of which they are now in possession.' A comparison of London tea prices with those in Hamburg and New York clearly demonstrated that 'the monopoly of the tea trade enjoyed by the East India Company costs the people of this country, on average, not less than two millions two hundred thousand pounds sterling a year!' In 1828 a committee claimed that the nefarious activities of the East India Company had depressed the annual consumption of duty-paid tea per person in Britain from twenty-eight ounces in 1800 to twenty ounces in 1828; a terrible state of affairs given that tea was one 'of the principal necessaries of life'. Even tea consumption in the 'poor convict population' of New South Wales, which conducted direct trade with China, was more than three times higher than among the 'free and wealthy people of Great Britain'. Its conclusion was that 'in the United Kingdom, where the Company have a complete monopoly, they fleece their countrymen of the last penny they can give'.

The situation was not made any easier by the company's paramilitary role and status. We have seen how Charles II allowed the company the option to deploy military force where necessary to secure trade; the result was a series of fortified trading stations in India. But in the eighteenth century the political landscape changed: the sway of the Mughal Emperor in Delhi was declining, replaced by a number of powerful regional princes. In retaliation, the East India Company turned to its army to restore government control over large swathes of India with the result that, at the dawn of the nineteenth century, reinforced by the British Army, the company dominated over half of India. Effectively, India, then, was ruled by twenty-four traders sitting in the East India Company boardroom in Leadenhall St. Many in Britain were uncomfortable with this blurring of the lines between flag and trade; the two should be mutually exclusive. One commentator in 1831 spoke for many when he wrote that 'we object to their being allowed to combine in their own persons the separate and irreconcilable functions of tea-dealers and rulers of a mighty empire. Let them make their election; let them choose as to whether they will be grocers or emperors; but do not allow them to attempt both ... To be a good grocer or a cheesemonger, a man must be nothing else. If the Company prefer these useful functions to those of a loftier character, we shall not blame them for their choice. But we protest against their being allowed to carry a sword in one hand and a ledger in the other – to act at once as sovereigns and tea dealers.'

The new company charter did away with its trading functions in China, making it an agent of the British government with responsibility for administering British India for the Crown from the boardroom of the East India Company. However, the twenty-four gentlemen ensconced there now had to focus on how best to replace their revenue streams. It was then that cultivating tea in India and Ceylon emerged as a real possibility.

Tea from India and Ceylon

Expeditious delivery to market, then, was not the only commercial consequence of the deregulation of the tea trade. The East India Company now had to compete with any number of companies for the right to import tea from China. Before now there was no commercial benefit in seeking new sources for tea; they had enjoyed the exclusive rights to the Chinese harvests and they could take as long as they liked shipping it back to the London market. In any event, tea from China was thought, conveniently for the complacency camp, to be the best in the world.

Trading tea in China had never been easy for the company. Apart from the usual bureaucracy and corruption involved in price, duty, taxes and the like, traders had to negotiate the Byzantine machinations of the Co-Hong – a seventeen-man monopoly based in Canton and neighbouring Whampoa though which all tea trade had to pass agonisingly until 1771 – eerily reminiscent in some ways of the comfortable monopolistic set-up enjoyed by the East India Company in London. The Hong (it means merchant in English) exacted an expensive insurance levy, payable in the inconceivable event of it going out of business, and demanded a margin of between 25 and 30 per cent on all deals. After 1771 a commercial cabal of thirteen Chinese merchants replaced the Hong; they could trade independently, thus permitting a greater chance of fairness. Business was further complicated by language; few English spoke good enough Chinese and vice versa, meaning that all transactions were conducted through interpreters. The situation was exacerbated because any Chinaman found teaching Chinese to a foreigner was subject to summary execution. Much of the 'interpretation' could only be described as 'loose', giving opportunities for yet more corruption on the part of the Chinese. The situation was not helped by acute cultural differences: the Chinese regarded the traders as *Untermenschen*, and barbarians; they called the trade 'tribute' to reinforce their fantasy of racial superiority. The traders, for their part, believed the Chinese to be godless and incorrigibly corrupt. Violence was often the result: one English merchant, Charles Compton, habitually gave any 'inconvenient' Chinese 'a good thrashing' – the Chinese responded in kind. William Melrose himself watched as the Chinese once razed to the ground English, Dutch and Greek factories. The intractable Compton narrowly escaped death when an angry mob were set on killing 'the foreign devils'; they burnt down the factory belonging to his Hong merchant when he and the Chinaman were still inside. Piracy was an additional and constant problem, sometimes resulting in fatalities on one or both sides.

In the event, the East India Company needed to look no further than their own comfort zone. India was their home ground, their overseas headquarters as both a commercial and a governmental entity. A tea committee was set up in Delhi to establish where in India tea might be best cultivated using seed imported from China, and to manage cultivation. Its mission statement read 'a plan for the establishment of tea culture in India'. The obvious region was Assam, where indigenous tea plants had already been found growing in the 1820s. Chinese seeds were duly germinated in Calcutta and then cultivated in trials in Assam and other potentially suitable areas. It was a Major Robert Bruce who set up the early plantations, declaring later in 1838 that Assam 'appears to me to be one big Tea country'. His brother, C. A. Bruce, who had resigned his commission with a gunboat flotilla to become agent for the East India Company in Assam, was now appointed Superintendent of Tea Forests and started the cultivation of Chinese tea. An agricultural disaster: the Chinese plants cross-pollinated with the indigenous tea plants. Bruce took the initiative and planted a nursery comprising only indigenous plants. In 1836, he sent a sample of his tea to the tea committee in Delhi. It won the approval of Lord Auckland, who considered it 'of good quality'; *Camellia sinensis var. assamica* was born. The following year Bruce sent a consignment to the committee comprising forty-six chests of indigenous tea. In 1839 twelve chests of Assam tea were sent to the East India Company in London. Some were used as sales samples, the rest went to the London Tea Auction – the first auction of Indian tea in Britain. A good price was obtained; Bruce's initiative was a huge agricultural and commercial success. The Assam Company was set up to manage, promote and expand Britain's Indian tea business. Problems there were many, including capturing and training elephants to carry tea through the jungles; nevertheless, by 1855 tea production in Assam exceeded half a million pounds in weight. Production was on a truly prodigious scale – factories were huge, plantations draped miles and miles of hillsides, tea was plucked by armies of labourers who had been rounded up by the 'coolie catchers' to work seven-year contracts in what amounted to slavery, living in cramped and insanitary conditions on the edges of the plantations. And this some years after the Slavery Abolition Act 1833 was passed, abolishing slavery throughout the British Empire – but the abolition was not without insidious exceptions: 'the Territories in the Possession of the East India Company', the 'Island of Ceylon', and 'the Island of Saint Helena'. These exceptions were annulled in 1843. The favourable economies of scale led to lower prices for tea from Assam and, later, from Darjeeling and Ceylon.

'So I says "My dear if you could give me a cup of tea to clear my muddle of a head I should better understand your affairs." And we had the tea and the affairs too ...'
Charles Dickens (1812–1870), *Mrs. Lirriper's Legacy*

In 1865 a paltry 3 per cent of tea came from India. By 1900 that had risen to 55 per cent, with Ceylon contributing a further 35 per cent; China was left with just over 7 per cent. By 1888 British tea imports from India exceeded those from China for the first time, and by 1898 tea exports from the subcontinent were fourteen times those from China: 219,000 pounds in weight against 15,678,000 pounds. Prices could be reduced further when merchants such as Thomas Lipton cut out the middlemen when he bought four estates, enabling him to boast 'Direct from the tea Gardens to the Tea Pot' in his advertising.

Ceylon also became an important producer. It was renowned originally for its cinnamon and coffee growing, until a serious fungus blight around 1865 known locally as 'devastating Emily' put an end to the coffee and forced Dr G. H. L. Thwaites, superintendent of the world-renowned Peradeniya Botanical Gardens, to experiment with alternative crops; the result was James Taylor's extensive Loolecondera Tea Estate, established in Kandy in 1867. Before that, Chinese seeds had been sown on the Rothschild estate in 1841: coffee covered 275,000 acres, tea 1,000. After the blight, in 1875, tea covered 384,000 acres. Between 1873 and 1880, thanks to Taylor, production rocketed from just 23 pounds to 81.3 tons, and by 1890, to 22,899.8 tons.

Mazawattee, Lipton, Ridgways, Brooke Bond and Teetgen all moved in and shipped tea out. In 1877, the first cargo of Ceylon tea reached London. Paying homage to Ceylon's valiant agricultural resurgence, Sir Arthur Conan Doyle noted that 'not often is it that men have the heart when their one great industry is ruined, to rear up in a few years another as rich to take it's place; and the tea fields of Ceylon are as true a monument to courage as is the lion of Waterloo'.

From 1880 Henry Randolph Trafford pioneered the conversion of coffee estates to tea plantations and thus boosted production further. Technology was not far behind: the first 'Sirocco' tea drier, made by Samuel Cleland Davidson in 1877, and the first tea-rolling machine, by John Walker & Co. in 1880, soon found their way to Ceylon. The Central Tea Factory in Nuwara Eliya was built in 1884, the first of many. Machinery from the United Kingdom – Marshals of Gainsborough, the Tangyes Machine Company of Birmingham, and Davidsons of Belfast – was imported to keep the Ceylon tea industry state of the art. The first public Colombo Tea Auction was held on 30 July 1883.

One million packets of tea were sold at the Chicago World's Fair in 1893; a record price of £36.15 per lb was set at the London Tea Auctions in the same year. In 1851, when all tea coming in to Britain originated from China, annual consumption per head was less than two pounds in weight. By 1901, the cheaper imports from India and Ceylon were responsible for a rise to over six pounds per head.

'We returned into the Castle, where we found Miss Skiffins preparing tea. The responsibility of making toast was delegated to the Aged. The Aged prepared such a haystack of buttered toast, that I could scarcely see him over it ... while Miss Skiffins prepared such a jorum of tea, that the pig in the back premises became strongly excited ... We ate the whole of the toast, and drank tea in proportion, and it was delightful to see how warm and greasy we all got after it.' Charles Dickens (1812–1870), *Great Expectations*

Tea Dealers and Grocers

As one of twenty-five York tea dealers in 1818, and importers of tea, coffee and chocolate, the Tukes were the sole holders in the north of England of a licence which permitted the processing of coffee beans and the sale of roasted coffee, tea and chocolate in the north. Between 1841 and 1863 the annual consumption of tea in Britain doubled, and so, therefore, did imports and the number of outlets. To put it into context, the tea dealers rubbed shoulders in York with eleven confectioners, seven fruiterers, forty-six grocers (who would also have sold tea), sixteen liqueur merchants and 184 inns. During the century tea had become a part of the stock in trade of the high-street grocer, reflecting the fact that tea was a staple on the 'shopping list' of his customers. The nine types of tea in a typical grocer's-cum-tea-dealer-cum fruiterer (T. Johnson in Colliergate) competed with 135 other lines, from coffee and sugar to snuff and soap, from Carolina rice, Turkey figs and cloves to mace and Barcelona nuts. In 1878 Julius Drewe established his Willow Pattern Tea Stores in Liverpool, soon extending to a chain which he called the Home & Colonial Stores, majoring in tea. By 1890 he had forty-three branches all over Britain. In Elizabeth Gaskell's *Cranford*, published in 1853, the unfortunate Miss

Matty is urged to consider tea dealing as a new occupation, if she 'could get over the degradation of condescending to anything like trade'. In 1872 the London Genuine Tea Company recruited sub-postmasters to act as their door-to-door salesmen. In 1824 John Cadbury had opened his tea, coffee and cocoa shop in Bull Street, Birmingham, after apprenticeships first at John Cudworth's grocers in Leeds, and then in London at the East India Company's bonded warehouse and at the Sanderson, Fox & Company teahouse. In York Joseph Rowntree Sr lays down the law for apprentices in their shop in Pavement: 'The object of the Pavement establishment is business. The young men who enter it ... are expected to contribute ... in making it successful ... it affords a full opportunity for any painstaking, intelligent young man to obtain a good practical acquaintance with the tea and grocery trades ... the place is not suitable for the indolent and wayward.'

Joseph Rowntree's grocery shop was but one of forty-nine grocers-cum-tea dealers in the city in 1851. His *Note on the taking & setting up of Orders [Important to all]* is typically scrupulous and illustrates the complexity of tea dealing: 'Be explicit in stating the particular kind of article wanted: e.g. if Coffee is ordered, state on order, whether whole, ground, mixed or genuine is wanted. – if Tea, - Black, Mixed, Assam, or whole-leaf: if Sugar, Lump, Raw or Moist.'

In 1862 Henry Rowntree made the decision to purchase the tea, coffee, cocoa and chicory business owned by the Tuke family. This was the start of the Rowntree chocolate business run by his brother, Joseph Rowntree Jr, until the 1920s. Tuke then moved the tea dealership part of his business to London – Tukes & Co., 20 Fenchurch Street near Mincing Lane – and eventually, in June 1862, sold it to John Casson. In the early twentieth century it became Tuke Mennell & Co., Wholesale Tea and Coffee Dealers, at Great Tower Street, London, separating in 1923.

Tea and Slavery

For reasons more down to geography than anything else, tea largely escaped direct involvement in the hideous slave trade, but sugar did not. Sweet-toothed British tea drinkers had a predilection for adding sugar to their tea – that sugar was harvested on the other side of the world to tea, relying on slave labour, that is, the men, women and children working on the plantations dehumanised as the 'Black Cattle'. The human cost of providing the tea drinker with his or her sweetener of choice is forever immortalised in Voltaire's *Candide* when the maimed slave points out, 'It is at this price that you eat sugar in Europe.' The abolitionists orchestrated a campaign to boycott West Indian slave-grown sugar, noting that Britain consumed more sugar than the rest of Europe put together (much of it dissolving in tea) and that if a family using five pounds a week used no sugar for twenty-one months it would prevent the murder or enslavement of one fellow human being. Abstention by 38,000 families would stop the trade altogether. Sugar was bigger than grain by 1750; there were 120 sugar refineries in Britain turning out 30,000 tons every year. In 1791 the abolitionist movement could count on 30,000 families joining the tea boycott. Tea-parties were held all over the country using cups and saucers decorated with anti-slavery images and slogans. The sceptre of slave labour still hovers over the tea trade today, notably in the tea plantations of India.

4

Drugs, Wars and Votes for Women

The Boston Tea Party

As we have seen, smuggling punctured the revenue and profits of the British East India Company. Add to this the financially embarrassing seventeen-million-pound surplus worth more than £2 million stockpiled by the company, and there comes an urgent need to find a market, preferably one not plagued by smugglers and pirates. If the East India Company failed, then so would the banks and the Treasury. The obvious market in which to offload was America, a British colony in which tea was consumed as avidly as it was in the motherland. The company sought leave from the British government to export tea direct to America, and the George III government, influenced no doubt by the £1 million debt owed to them by the company and reluctant to see it and the Treasury go under, agreed and imposed a tax of 3d per pound under the Tea Act. The colonists received this with rage, believing such an imposition to be illegal. *The Massachusetts Gazette* boomed that anyone assisting the East India Company would be considered an 'enemy of America'. Four ships, the *Dartmouth*, *Eleanor*, *Beaver* and *William*, duly arrived in Boston harbour in December 1733 laden with tea, only to be met with furious and defiant crowds of colonists. They blockaded the cargoes, refusing to allow them to be offloaded, they blockaded the ships, preventing them from leaving the harbour, and, dressed up as Mohawk Indians, eventually consigned the tea, all 342 chests of it, to the bottom of the harbour. The words 'Let every man do his duty, and be true to his country' were spoken and heard; there was no violence, except to the tea, and the Americans even swept up after them. Fish subsequently caught in the harbour tasted strongly of tea.

The outrage and the sabotage was over a matter of principle; in fact, the duty and the cost of the tea were both considerably less than what prevailed in Britain. It was the principle of 'no taxation without representation' that the colonists clamoured to uphold.

Boston was the catalyst for more protests. In retaliation, the British government passed the 1774 Intolerable Acts, which achieved little other than to unite the thirteen American colonies against British rule. In September 1774 the First Continental Congress convened to agree resistance against the Acts, leading to the Declaration of Independence in July 1776, three years after the Boston Tea Party.

The Opium Wars: 1839 to 1842, 1856 to 1860

The British East India Company was implicated in the drug running and drug addiction that characterised Britain's war with China over the opium trade. For 1,000 years opium was used in China for medicinal purposes. In the seventeenth century that changed, when Europeans introduced the Chinese to the less-than-healthy practice of mixing opium with tobacco for smoking. Non-medicinal consumption of opium was outlawed by the Yongzheng Emperor in 1729 but to no avail: in 1729 annual imports of opium into China were 200 chests, by 1800 the figure was 4,500 chests, and in 1838, on the eve of the first Opium War, it was 40,000 chests. Where was it all coming from? From the East India Company's factories in Bengal, Patna and Benares, and from Malwa in the non-British controlled parts of India.

After the Battle of Plassey in 1757 Britain annexed Bengal and the British East India Company assumed a monopoly on production and export of Indian opium. From about 1773 to 1823 opium was vital to the East India Company's governance of India. Opium smuggling had become one of the world's most valuable single-commodity trades; it has been dubbed 'the most long continued and systematic international crime of modern times' by John K. Fairbanks, in *The Creation of the Treaty System*. In a bid to reduce the huge trade deficit that had opened up between Britain and China, the East India Company started counter-trading Indian opium in return for tea. This also served to increase smuggled imports of opium into China. The company looked both ways – trading legally in upfront markets, while covertly exploiting illicit ones. British merchants bought tea in Canton on credit, paying for it by auctioning opium in Calcutta with the proviso it was sent to China. From there, the opium would be smuggled into China aboard British ships via traffickers and agency houses such as Jardine, Matheson & Co. and Dent & Co. The shocking bottom line was that most of the tea consumed in Britain at this time was paid for with opium.

'Corney was about to solace herself with a cup of tea. As she glanced from the table to the fireplace, where the smallest of all possible kettles was singing a small song in a small voice, her inward satisfaction evidently increased ... thrusting a silver spoon (private property) into the inmost recesses of a two-ounce tin tea-caddy proceeded to make the tea.' Charles Dickens (1812–1870), *Oliver Twist*

Daoguang, the Qing Dynasty emperor, sent Lin Zexu to Guangzhou, where in March 1839, acting on moral and social grounds, he arrested over 1,700 Chinese opium dealers and confiscated over 70,000 opium pipes. When he tried to get foreign companies to give up their opium for tea, and failed, Lin resorted to force, blockading the foreigners in their factories. Within six weeks the merchants surrendered 2.6 million pounds in weight of opium for destruction; this amounted to nearly a year's supply. Five hundred workers toiled for twenty-three days from 3 June, mixing it with lime and salt before dumping it into the sea. 26 June is now the International Day against Drug Abuse and Illicit Trafficking, held in honour of Lin Zexu's work.

The British responded by starting the First Opium War in 1839, raiding the Chinese coast. The outcome was that Britain wrested Hong Kong from China, along with some trade concessions in the Treaty of Nanking – known as the Unequal Treaties – which marked the start of China's 'Century of Humiliation'. After China's defeat in the Second Opium War of 1858, Britain forced China to legalise opium under the Tientsin Treaties, which resulted in massive domestic production and imports. In 1858, about twenty years after the First Opium War, annual imports rose to 70,000 chests (4,480 tons), equivalent to the global production of opium in the ten years either side of 2000. In 1879 it had risen to 6,700 tons. By 1906 China was producing 85 per cent of the world's opium, about 35,000 tons, and 27 per cent of its adult male population were frequent opium users – 13.5 million opium-dependent people consuming 35,000 tons of opium each year.

Three of a series of postcards released by Lipton's, depicting their tea operations in Ceylon. These show tea picking on a Ceylon tea estate, transportation of tea from a tea estate, and a street scene in Colombo.

The Rise of the Tea Room and the Women's Suffrage Movement

We have seen how, by the 1880s, tea rooms became popular and fashionable, especially with women who now had a respectable place in which they could meet, chat and relax in safety, with dignity and in comfort. In her online article 'Tea and Women – How the Tearoom Supported Women's Suffrage', Jane Pettigrew points out how many local branches of the Suffragette movement evolved from local temperance societies. Tea was served at these meetings, where attendees were urged to reject alcohol and drink 'the cup that cheers but does not inebriate'. But, apart from this rather ad hoc, transient accommodation, there was nowhere suitable for middle-class, politically motivated, independent-minded women to meet. Even everyday shoppers had a problem: the entrepreneur William Whiteley (1831–1907) opened his famous Whiteley's department store in Bayswater in 1870 and applied for a licence for an in-store restaurant; he was refused because it might attract 'immoral assignations'. The self-styled 'Universal Provider' could literally provide 'everything from a pin to an elephant', but he could not offer a restaurant or a refreshment room for his shoppers. All was not lost, though – in 1893 Derry & Toms of Kensington High Street had the vision to open a sumptuous tea room, redolent of a cosy home, to keep women in the store and allow them to spend more money.

> '[Maggy] must stop at a grocer's window ... for her to show her learning. She stumbles through various philanthropic recommendations to "Try our Mixture, Try our Family Black, try our orange-flavoured Pekoe, challenging competition at the head of Flowery Teas; and various cautions to the public against spurious establishments and adulterated articles."' Charles Dickens (1812–1870), *Little Dorrit*

No doubt Derry & Toms offered facilities – generally speaking, though, women's toilets were rather thin on the ground – the provision of which was considered by some a truly preposterous suggestion. It was only contested in 1884, when the Ladies Lavatory Company opened the first 'convenience' near Oxford Circus. By 1938 things had moved on enough for Blackpool Woolworth's ladies' public toilet to incorporate a kiosk selling sanitary towels, among other female necessities. The need to cater for the increasingly mobile and un-chaperoned woman had begun to be recognised, albeit in a limited way. Women-only clubs started to spring up – The University Women's Club was founded by a Girton graduate in 1883 in Audley Square, London W1. It offered a dining room, dressing room, drawing room, and library. Women may not have been able to gain a degree at Oxford but they could get a cup of tea in W1. In 1898 the Camelot Club in Queen Square, London WC1, provided for female shop and office workers. Harrods Ladies' Club, founded in 1890, was particularly revolutionary: apart from the silk decoration, marble, stained glass, and Indian carpets, a fully staffed nursery looked after the customers' children from 1921. In London's Mortimer Street there was the university graduate Somerville Club at No. 21 above the ABC tea shop, the Welbeck Restaurant at No. 44 which provided 'good, cheap food' for working-class girls, and one of the chain of Dorothy Restaurants at No. 81, run by women for women, which stayed open until

10 p.m. In Sheffield, the Howard Street Club provided for women workers in the silver and cutlery trades from 1914.

But it was the tea rooms that were the most popular with women – they were the perfect place for a discreet chat and discussions, which for some would have included politics and the vexed question of votes for women, and the necessary strategy, campaigns and demonstration necessary to achieve their goals. Roger Fulford sums up the situation in his *Votes For Women*: 'The spread of independence was helped by the growth of the tea-shop. A few expensive restaurants existed but apart from these ... there were no places for a quick meal; [the tea-room] was an integral part of the women's liberation movement.'

> David was 'steeped in Dora'. 'How many cups of tea I drank, because Dora made it, I don't know. But I perfectly remember that I sat swilling tea until my whole nervous system, if I had any in those days, must have gone by the board.' Charles Dickens (1812–1870), *David Copperfield*

The tea shops run by the ABC (Aerated Bread Company) accommodated this new-found social freedom; according to suffragist Margery Corbett Ashby (1882–1981) they were 'an enormous move to freedom'. The first opened in 1884, and there were over fifty just six years later; the Lyons restaurants began opening from 1894. In 1907, the Young Hot Bloods, younger members of the militant 1907 Women's Social & Political Union led by Emmeline and Christabel Pankhurst, met at a tea shop in the Strand. Alan's Tea Room at 263 Oxford Street allowed free use of its spacious function room for members of the Women's Social & Political Union, as first advertised in the WSPU newspaper, *Votes for Women*, on 31 December 1908. The room was used in 1910 by the Tax Resistance League conference and in 1911 by the Catholic Women's Suffrage Society for its inaugural meeting. The Forward Cymric Union – a militant Welsh suffrage society – held its monthly meetings there around 1912; on 26 July 1913, at the end of the NUWSS Suffrage Pilgrimage, Margory Lees and her friends dined there. The proprietor, always assumed to be a man, Mr Alan Liddle, turned out to be Miss Marguerite Alan Liddle (1873–1946), the sister of Helen Gordon Liddle, an active member of the Women's Social and Political Union and author of *The Prisoner*, a memoir of the month she spent in Strangeways Prison, Manchester, in October 1909. 'Alan' had plenty of competition: a Lipton refreshment room at Nos 265–7, another restaurant at 269, a Lyons tea room at 277–81 and an ABC at 283. An advertisement in 1910 in the 'Vanity Pages' of *The Idler*, a magazine edited by Jerome K. Jerome, gives a picture (literally) of Alan's, in what amounts to an early version of a text message with a photo by a Mrs Edward Talbot, who called in while out clothes shopping:

> We then had the nicest little luncheon, with the comforting knowledge that everything was homemade, at Alan's Tea Rooms for the modest sum of ⅙. We send you a sketch and a menu, so you can see for yourself. The rooms are charmingly decorated; one is set apart for smoking, while another, which is large and sunny,

can be hired for At Homes and meetings. You can lunch, also, for a shilling, and for afternoon tea Alan's popularity is undoubted.

Mrs Talbot does not sound much like a militant but she may well have rubbed shoulders with a few suffragettes during that enjoyable lunchtime.

The writer Elizabeth Crawford has done much original research uncovering the important role the tea shops played in the suffragette movement; it is published in her web-based articles under the title 'Woman and Her Sphere' and provides the basis for much of what follows. For example, we learn how Kate Frye joined a meeting in a Lyons tea room close to Parliament Square on 21 November 1911 with other suffragettes to plan an evening smashing the windows of government offices. Outside London there was much tea-shop militancy: in Newcastle, Fenwick's café was frequented by Dr Ethel Bentham and Lisbeth Simm, who formed the 'Drawing-Room Café' meetings, a forum in which women met to discuss political issues. In Nottingham the WSPU convened at Morley's Café, a temperance establishment; The Café Vegetaria in Edinburgh was the place to go for local Women's Freedom League Society – this is where on the night of 2 April 1911 suffragettes met to evade the census enumerator.

Somewhat perversely, in 1912 tea rooms were among the targets of the March 1912 WSPU window-smashing campaign. Victims included ABC tea rooms in The Strand and in Bond Street. 'Suffragette friendly' tea rooms were increasingly used as venues for protest – some ad hoc, some orchestrated. On 20 December 1913 a suffragette in the Eustace Miles restaurant delivered a speech criticising the government's treatment of suffragette prisoners. Asked to sit down, she was nevertheless allowed to continue with her meeting, more discreetly. On the same day, at Fuller's in Regent Street, a woman addressed her captive audience from the gallery while two others dropped leaflets; they were asked to leave. When, a few days later, there was a second scene at Fuller's, the orchestra drowned out the speaker. *The Suffragette* reported how in a Lyons Corner House a woman stood up to speak, receiving applause and heckling alike. Lyons security men manhandled her out of the building despite opposition from other guests; in the end she made a dignified exit to a chorus of 'Isn't she plucky'.

An advertisement for the Teacup Inn ran 'Dainty luncheons and Afternoon teas at moderate charges. Home cookery. Vegetarian dishes and sandwiches. Entirely staffed and managed by women.' It was opened in January 1910 in Portugal Street off Kingsway. Mrs Hansell, the owner, promoted the Tea Cup Inn in *Votes for Women* – emphasising its proximity to the WSPU office in Clement's Inn, and in 1912 it was even closer when it moved to Lincoln's Inn House in Kingsway. The London Opera House opened in November 1911 across the road in Portugal Street and was used as a venue for many a suffragette meeting.

Suffragette societies, of course, ran fundraising events in their shops and at bazaars – they even commissioned the special china in which to serve their tea. One of the best-known events is the WSPU Exhibition held at the Prince's Skating Rink at Knightsbridge in May 1909. The tea room there was run by Mrs Henrietta Lowy and her four daughters along with another young suffragette, Una Dugdale. The Staffordshire pottery H. M. Williamson of Longton was engaged to make the china. Each of the twenty-two pieces of the tea service was decorated with Sylvia Pankhurst's motif, the 'Angel of Freedom'; behind this and the familiar banner and trumpet, the initials 'WSPU' were highlighted

Sylvia Pankhurst (third from the right, seated) and fellow suffragettes celebrating with a cup of tea in the East End of London. Originally published in *Picture Post*.

Various tea products produced for the troops fighting in the Boer War and First World War. The T(tea) M(milk) S(sugar) tablets were sent to soldiers in the trenches by John Richardson & Co. Leicester Ltd: 'Each tablet contains compressed tea and milk, sufficiently sweetened for an ordinary cup. Directions – thoroughly powder the tablet before adding the boiling water.'

against dark prison bars, garlanded by thistle, shamrock, rose and dangling chains. At the end of the exhibition, the services were sold off. The WSPU not only sold the china, they sold their own brand of tea as well, as frequently advertised in *Votes for Women*.

'My hour for tea is half-past five, and my buttered toast waits for nobody.' Wilkie Collins (1824–1899)

Tea and the World Wars

In the First World War the 12,000 officers and 320,000 men (the size of the entire British Army originally sent over to France and Belgium) of the Army Service Corps had the unenviable task of catering for the 5 million British troops, 3 million of whom were on the Western Front, on an everyday basis. In 1914 the daily ration included ⅝ oz of tea; other beverages issued were ¹/10 gill of lime juice (where fresh vegetables were not issued) and ½ gill of rum at the discretion of the battalion commander. Some of these officers were teetotal and prohibited their men from having any. The Germans, on the other hand, could ⅚ enjoy ⁹/10 oz of coffee, or ¹/10 oz of tea; the commanding officer dispensed 0.17 of a pint of spirits, 0.44 of a pint of wine, or 0.88 of a pint of beer at his discretion. British troops fighting in India received 1 oz of tea, Indian troops ⅓ oz. On the home front rationing was introduced at the end of 1917 as U-boats made it increasingly difficult to import sufficient food and drink, so tea prices increased. The government bought up tea stocks to control supply. Typhoo were none too pleased at this; they were trading in leaf-edge rather than regular tea, so they could not make their product from the tea the government intended to supply. An appeal signed by 4,000 medical scientists fell on deaf ears, and as a last resort the company inserted leaflets into their packs urging customers to complain and state the medical reason why they needed leaf-edge tea. The Tea Controller was overwhelmed but he finally relented and Typhoo tea was made freely available again. The ration was a mere two ounces per person per week, but the restriction could be legally avoided by those with lots of children; the parents could drink their allocation or benefit from those rations which went unclaimed. Sgt T. J. Williams of the 5th King's Own Lancashire Regiment tells the story, in Rowntree's *Cocoa Works Magazine* in 1915, of how a tin of tea nearly saved his life. During the Battle of St Julien he received a one pound tin of Rowntree's Elect, which he duly put in his emergency ration pack along with a tin of tea and sugar. 'Advancing under heavy fire and now and again dropping flat on the ground ... a bullet entered my valise ... [it] had gone through the tin containing the tea and sugar, the tin of Rowntrees had been penetrated on one side and not the other. What luck! ... If it had gone through it would have penetrated my back.' At the end of the war tea was an essential component of the street parties which were organised to celebrate peace.

The YMCA performed a crucial role during the war, dispensing refreshments and reading material for troops both at home and overseas. Within ten days of war being declared the YMCA had set up than 250 recreation centres in the United Kingdom, providing a cup of tea, sandwiches or other refreshments. These huts were sited near to railway stations and other places where troops congregated. In the war zones the 300 or so erected there could be found in the main Army bases, near field dressing stations and at railway junctions. Scout huts sprang up to perform a similar role – they offered facilities for amateur dramatics, with reading and writing rooms and a canteen in which some 900 men a day were served with tea, cocoa and cigarettes.

Tea was to serve a similar morale-boosting role, providing respite and reassurance for those on active service and those on the home front, during the Second World War. 'Tea is more important than bullets,' said Winston Churchill. To the historian A. A. Thompson, tea was England's secret weapon, 'What keeps 'em together is tea', 'em' being the armed services and the Women's Institute. Within two days of the declaration of war against Germany, the government requisitioned all tea stocks and dispersed the supplies around the country to spare them from destruction by German bombing. Rationing was introduced in 1940 in response to the German naval blockades: two ounces of tea per person per week for those over the age of five, enough for two or three cups a day of weak tea. Those in the armed forces, and anyone working in crucial industries at home, were allocated more. The Red Cross sent tea in Red Cross parcels to British prisoners of war abroad. The teahouses of J. Lyons & Co. squeezed 100 cups of tea to the pound rather than the usual eighty-five, and the Oxford Street Corner House stayed open throughout the Blitz except for three days in September 1940 when they had no water supply, but even then the 'Front Shop' managed to continue trading. A tea shop menu from the time lists tea at 3*d* per cup or 4*d* per pot (per person), with scones at a penny halfpenny. In the early 1990s Lyons sent out an appeal for ex-'Nippies', as Lyons waitresses were affectionately called, to send in their memories. One lady who did, Mrs

The famous mirror in Bettys, York, on which some 500 members of the Royal Canadian Air Force stationed around York etched their names while on a night off. Many did not live to see the end of the war.

Edith Walsh from Streatham, as recorded in *Sources for the History of London 1939–45*, worked at the largest of the Brixton tea shops in 1941. Arriving for work one morning after a raid they opened up the shop ...

> Word soon got round that Lyons were open and serving food and drink (we had our own generators). It seemed that the world and his wife came into our shop that day. Mrs Hedley (our manageress) told us not to try to keep to our own 'stations,' just give the people the drinks and food as the counter-hands placed it out for us. The teashop was so crowded we couldn't recognise who we'd 'put what down for' so we just gave a bill for what we thought was OK. That night we couldn't believe how many bill books we'd used and how much adding up we had to do from the slips at the top. As you can imagine our commission was the best we ever had.

> '"Have some wine", the March hare said in an encouraging tone. Alice looked all round the table, but there was nothing on it but tea. "I don't see any wine", she remarked. "There isn't any", said the March hare ... "Take some more tea" the March Hare said to Alice, very earnestly. "I've had nothing yet," Alice replied in an offended tone, "so I can't take more." "You mean you can't take less," said the Hatter: "it's very easy to take more than nothing."' Lewis Carroll (1832–1898), *Alice's Adventures in Wonderland*

As with many companies, Lyons's factories were given over to the war effort: they transformed into one of the UK's largest bomb-making facilities, while their engineering works made other war materiel in a factory at Elstow near Bedford. They sent millions of ration packs to troops in Asian and other theatres of war, and handed over one of their tea shops to American personnel stationed around Grosvenor Square; another formed part of Rainbow Corner in Shaftsbury Avenue. Mazawattee tea was sold in gas-proof (hermetically sealed) tins and a new-fangled product, the TeaFuse, was sold with the slogan: 'Increase your tea ration.'

Twinings supplied tea for those Red Cross packages, for the Women's Voluntary Service, and for many YMCA wartime canteens. When their tea shop on the Strand was bombed, they had the tables set back up within hours to continue service. Included in the 20 million Red Cross parcels was a quarter of a pound of tea. Tea rationing prevailed until October 1952, but was lifted in good time for Elizabeth II's coronation the following year, which could now be celebrated properly with a very British cup of tea. Tea had other, less tasty wartime functions, such as women washing rare stockings in leftover tea to keep their colour, and using tea to dye their legs in place of stockings. Spent tea leaves were effective in removing scratches from brown floors, cold strained black tea worked with stained black silk dresses and muddy black shoes – all on the authority of *Home Chat* in July 1940.

On 3 April 1941 the RAF carried out one of its more appreciated raids: it dropped 75,000 tea bombs, bags of Dutch East Indies tea each containing about an ounce of the colony's finest tea, over the occupied Netherlands. Each bag was labelled with the Netherlands flag and the words, 'The Netherlands will rise again. Greetings from the

Tea helped sustain those on the front line during the Second World War, and those fighting on the home front, particularly during the Blitz. Here women of the Auxiliary Fire Service provide tea for firefighters during a break. Originally published in *The Home Front* (1947).

Free Netherlands East Indies. Chins Up.' The tea was a gift from Dutch East Indies tea planters; the reaction from the Dutch News Agency read, 'Never have the Dutch people so gratefully received a gift from the Dutch East Indies, especially as it is almost impossible to get an ounce of tea in the Dutch shops.'

The Waldorf in London was forced to suspend its popular tea dances in 1939 when a German bomb shattered the glass roof of the Palm Court; the dances were resumed in 1982. Another casualty of the bombing was Mincing Lane – the Street of Tea. Much of it was destroyed by bombs and incendiaries in 1940, and along with it many of the offices, archives, records and the warehouses of the tea trade companies which populated the area.

Tea and the 'Troubles'

When British troops disembarked in Belfast in 1969 they were welcomed by Protestants and Catholics alike – they signified protection against sectarian attacks. Soldiers were plied with tea and toast in the Catholic Falls Road area of west Belfast, and the images were shown all around the world and gave signs of hope.

However, the hospitality did not last for very long: Protestants soon saw the Army as their exclusive protectors against the Provisional IRA, while to many Catholics the Army was an oppressive force supporting unionist rule. Ken Wharton's acclaimed book *Bullets, Bombs and Cups Of Tea: Further Voices of the British Army in Northern Ireland 1969–98*, among other things, reaffirms in its title the importance of tea as a morale-booster and source of sustenance among British troops and British civilians in nearly thirty years of violence and fear. Ken Wharton was a door-to-door tea deliveryman for Rington's Tea before joining the Army in 1967 at the age of seventeen. One senior NCO tells, in John Lindsay's *Brits Speak Out: British Soldiers' Impressions of the Northern*

'When the girl returned, some hours later, she carried a tray, with a cup of fragrant tea steaming on it; and a plate piled up with very hot buttered toast, cut thick, very brown on both sides, with the butter running through the holes in it in great golden drops, like honey from the honeycomb. The smell of that buttered toast simply talked to Toad; and with no uncertain voice; talked of warm kitchens, of breakfasts on bright frosty mornings, of cosy parlour firesides on winter evenings, when one's ramble was over, and slippered feet were propped on the fender; of the purring of contented cats, and the twitter of sleepy canaries.' Kenneth Grahame (1859–1932), *The Wind in the Willows*

Ireland Conflict, how 'On the other [Republican] side, some of the people whose homes we'd have to search would be as nice as pie. Once the curtains were drawn they would chat to you and make you cups of tea.' Nothing exceptional about that you might say, but in Ireland, north and south, the cup of tea is a potent symbol of friendship and hospitality. Less attractively, British Army Royal Military Police 'investigations' into over 150 killings by the Army in the early 1970s were known as 'tea and sandwich inquiries', to mark the casual nature of the enquiries and the cosy relationship which existed between the RUC and the Army.

5

British Tea Culture

It was not long after tea drinking had been taken up in all sections of British society that it started to inform and infuse our culture. This chapter looks at a number of ways in which tea insinuated itself into the British way of life and established practices and institutions, many of which survive today. One way of looking at the essential 'Britishness' of tea drinking is to view it against the insistence on drinking coffee by our continental neighbours, to the virtual exclusion of tea. Richard Coulton's post, 'Milking It', on the *QM History of Tea Project* blog, features an anecdote which will be familiar to all:

> An older member of the party, tiring of the foreign insistence on serving coffee at all times of the day, would request a cup of tea from a waiter in a café or restaurant. After consulting with a colleague behind the bar, the member of staff would eventually return with a cup of lukewarm water, a bowl of sugar, and an individually wrapped Lipton Yellow Label tea-bag (a brand never knowingly encountered in the UK). To the incredulity of us Brits, milk was nowhere to be seen. Cue further faltering communication. Perhaps eventually there would emerge a small jug of UHT, usually served hotter than the water in which the Lipton was now dully infusing. The next time round, everyone stuck to coffee.
>
> 'Milking It', posted by Richard Coulton on 3 July, 2013

Afternoon Tea

The Duchess of Bedford, and her desire for snacking, is usually credited for the aristocratic ritual that became 'afternoon tea'. However, it seems that the powerful and influential supporter of Charles II, Elizabeth Maitland, Duchess of Lauderdale, preceded Bedford by some 160 years. In the opulent Ham House, her boudoir, the 'white closet', was furnished in the Japanese style ('six arme chayres Japand') and also featured 'one Indian furnace for tee garnished with silver'. Moreover, in the anteroom were 'six Japand backstools' and 'a Japan box for sweetmeats and tea' with 'a Tea table carv'd and guilt'. What was the Duchess of Lauderdale doing if she was not serving afternoon tea to her friends? The five unmarried daughters of the recently widowed Lady Alice Brownlow were holding a clandestine tea party in 1697 in Belton House when they heard their authoritarian mother approaching: the tea and all the paraphernalia were hastily thrown out of the window.

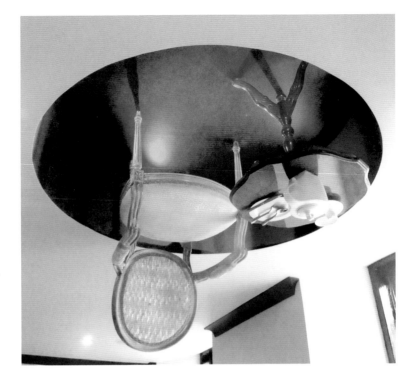

Just one of the quirky features of the *Alice in Wonderland-*themed Curious Tea Rooms in Frederick Street, Edinburgh.

Around 1841 Anna Maria Russell, the 7th Duchess of Bedford and Marchioness of Tavistock, was getting rather tired of the long wait for dinner: she had had breakfast some hours ago around 10 a.m. and was not due to eat again until 8 p.m. That late-afternoon 'sinking feeling' was plaguing her, so she took social convention into her own hands, made a pot of tea and a light snack, and consumed it in the privacy of her boudoir. From that moment on Anna, and thousands of well-to-do women like her, could be said to have 'lost that sinking feeling'. Such clandestine, solitary snacking was not to last; before long, invitations were going out to friends requesting their company in her rooms at Woburn Abbey. When she returned to fashionable, trend-setting London, cards went out to lady friends asking them to join her for 'tea and a walking the fields'. Afternoon tea quickly caught on and was deemed respectable enough to move downstairs into the drawing room. Mid-afternoon tea-drinking and sandwich-eating became all the rage. Afternoon tea was sometimes called 'low tea' after the low tables, coffee tables, indeed, on which it was served. Earlier references to afternoon tea are in Fanny Burney's *Evelina, or the History of a Young Lady's Entrance into the World* (1778): 'I was relieved by a summons to tea,' and by John Wesley in 1789: 'At breakfast and at tea ... I met all the Society.' Jane Austen is probably referring to high tea when she writes in 1803 in the unfinished *The Watsons*, 'The entrance of the tea-things at seven o'clock was some relief.'

The Wordsworths were big tea drinkers and so tea occurs often in Dorothy Wordsworth's *Journals*. On a trip to Scotland, near Loch Lomond, she writes, 'The hostess provided us with tea and sugar for our breakfast; the water was boiled in an iron pan, and dealt out to us in a jug, a proof that she does not often drink tea, though she said she had always tea and sugar in the house.' Distance was no object for those who could afford it: Dorothy was having '6lb of good West India coffee (roasted); 75lb of Souchong tea and of Congue' shipped up to the Lake District by canal around 1812. Tea was still very expensive – over seven shillings a pound – and at one time the Wordsworths owed Twinings over £4,000 for two years' supply – a phenomenal amount of money. Dorothy was famously thrifty: her used tea leaves were dried and given to the neighbours. She could have helped some of her neighbours even more by explaining how actually to take tea – writing in his *Commonplace Book* in 1850, Robert Southey describes the fate of the first pound of tea sent to Penrith: 'It was sent as a present without directions how to use it. They boiled the whole at once in a kettle, and sat down to eat the leaves with butter and salt; and they wondered how anyone could like such a dish.'

Afternoon tea drinking had already won for itself a reputation for gossip- and scandal-mongering. John Bowles' 1710 illustration is tagged with 'thick scandal circulates with right Bohea', while the devil sits under the tea table sipping his tea and a serpent-wielding demon banishes all that is good from the room. Jonathan Swift in his 1729 *The Journey of a Modern Lady* remarks that the hostess could find herself 'surrounded with the noisy clans of prudes, coquettes and harridans'. Dr Aiken, in the 1795 *The History of Manchester*, reminds us that tea was not to everyone's taste; a respectable and venerable old lady from Salford could not get on with the 'new-fashioned beverage of tea' and was always given her usual 'tankard of ale and pipe of tobacco' on social visits.

The Duchess of Bedford's friend Queen Victoria – for whom she had served as Lady of the Bedchamber – popularised tea taking when she formalised the ritual with her Buckingham Palace 'tea receptions', or Drawing Room Teas, at which up to 200 guests with an open 'at home' invitation could call in between 4 p.m. and 7 p.m. Dressing up in fine tea gowns, gloves and hats was obligatory. Al fresco afternoon tea was taken in tea gardens, and the migration of afternoon tea to expensive hotels like the Ritz

Staff from Harrogate, Starbeck, Leeds and Bradford congregating outside the original Bettys in Harrogate just before the 1931 outing to Windermere. Five charabancs carried around 120 members of staff to the Lake District. Owner Frederick Belmont can be seen at the front in the middle.

and the Waldorf gave rise to the tea dance, which survived into the Second World War. The author of the contemporary *Etiquette of Modern Society* rules that a thoughtful hostess should always provide biscuits with tea, since these can be eaten more easily than sandwiches and did not require one to remove one's gloves. Refinement and strictly observed etiquette were the orders of the day; afternoon tea was responsible for the rise of the cucumber sandwich, cutting the crusts off bread, using only the finest china, and the three-tiered cake plate. Indeed, the cucumber sandwich became a prerequisite of middle-class afternoon entertaining; in Oscar Wilde's *The Importance Of Being Earnest* from 1895 the obligatory cucumber sandwiches ordered for Lady Bracknell's visit for afternoon tea are all eaten by her nephew and host, Algernon Moncrieff, who, in league with his butler, pretends outrage and lies that 'there were no cucumbers in the market this morning ... not even for ready money'. Even schoolboys were caught up in the craze: in 1739 Richard How wrote to his mother from his school in Wandsworth, thanking her for the shirt but asking for some tea. In 1766 William Dutton wrote to his father from Eton asking him to send 'tea and sugar here to drink in the afternoon' with his trendy friends – a *sine qua non* of Eton life. The Anglophile Henry James opens his *Portrait of a Lady* in 1881 with a closely observed description of an al fresco English afternoon tea party that is nothing short of perfection, a utopia: 'There are few hours in life more agreeable than the hour dedicated to the ceremony known as afternoon tea ... From five o' clock to eight is on certain occasions a little eternity; but on such an occasion as this the interval could only be an eternity of pleasure.'

'It is very strange, this domination of our intellect by our digestive organs. We cannot work, we cannot think, unless our stomach wills so. It dictates to us our emotions, our passions. After eggs and bacon, it says, "Work!" After beefsteak and porter, it says, "Sleep!" After a cup of tea (two spoonfuls for each cup, and don't let it stand more than three minutes), it says to the brain, "Now, rise, and show your strength. Be eloquent, and deep, and tender; see, with a clear eye, into Nature and into life; spread your white wings of quivering thought, and soar, a god-like spirit, over the whirling world beneath you, up through long lanes of flaming stars to the gates of eternity!"' Jerome K. Jerome, *Three Men in a Boat (To Say Nothing of the Dog)*, 1889

But what of the lower orders? From the end of the eighteenth century, with the advent of the Industrial Revolution and the long days in the factories, the main meal moved from the middle of the day; working people made do with a more substantial 'high' tea at five or six o'clock. It was 'high' only because of the height of the dinner tables on which tea was served. High tea fitted in with the end of the working day, be it in field or factory, and set the worker up for the early start next morning. It was sometimes called 'meat tea' as meat was often served. As we have seen, La Rochefoucauld observed from Paris the ubiquity of tea across all society.

Worthies from the upper classes sneered; Scottish Duncan Forbes said in 1744 that 'when tea and Punch became this the Diet and Debauch of all the beer and Ale drinkers, the Effects were suddenly and severely felt'. Jonas Hanway concurred; 'The Use of

A delightful 1940s card showing mother studiously being mum. The artist is Gladys Emma Peto (1890–1977), artist, fashion designer, illustrator and children's author. She is remembered as one of our best-known illustrators of fashionable life. Courtesy of Jane Pettigrew.

Tea descended to the Pleboean order among us ... it is the curse of the nation, that the labourer and mechanic will ape the lord.' Tea, though, was here to stay for all classes. Some of the wealthy paid their maids a weekly tea allowance; Jane Dowie in 1780 Devon received £1.6/- for nine months. An incredulous Italian visitor in 1755 spluttered that the maids' allowances amounted to the total wage of servants in Italy. The absence of tea as a perk even became a resigning issue, as this 1801 letter to the *Lady's Monthly Museum or Polite Repository* tells us: 'Her only reason for quitting being that her mistress did not suffer her to drink tea twice a day.' William Kitchiner attempted to formalise things in 1823 when he recorded in *The Cook's Guide* that maids receive half a pound of tea per month paid in lieu of wages valued at £3 10s, along with sugar, shoes, stockings, gowns, a bonnet, shawl, needles and scissors. In 1767 Arthur Young had noticed that farm labourers had the temerity to down tools and demand tea for their breakfasts with the maids. David Davies, a Berkshire rector, asked in his *The Case of the Labourers in Husbandry* in 1795 'why should such people ... indulge in a luxury which is only proper for their betters?' Tea for the good rector was 'a miserable infusion'.

In Wales, during times of austerity, village women joined tea clubs, Clwb Te, and pooled money and equipage. Marie Trevelyan, in her *Folk-lore and folk-stories of Wales*, tells us how in 1893 one woman would bring the tea, one the cake and another the gin or brandy to fortify it; 'They visited the homes of the members in turn, and naturally gossiped about what interested women.' In working-class England, Elizabeth Gaskell's character the mother of Mary Barton prefers 'sixpennyworth of rum to warm tea'. In

Scotland, an article in an 1853 edition of the *Edinburgh Review* describes how tea can have an uplifting and cheering effect on the elderly and lonely:

> by her fireside ... the lonely widow sits; the kettle simmers over the ruddy embers, and the blackened teapot on the hot brick prepares her evening drink ... as she sips the warm beverage ... genial thoughts awaken in her mind; her cottage grows less dark and lonely, and comfort seems to enliven the ill-furnished cabin.

Workhouse fare also included tea and sugar, with an allowance of 1 oz of tea for the over sixties in Aberystwyth and a pint of tea for breakfast for the under sixties. Tea provision generally in workhouses may have something to do with the philanthropist Louisa Twining; born 1820 as the ninth and youngest child of Richard Twining, she founded the Workhouse Visiting Society in 1859.

'We had a kettle; we let it leak: Our not repairing it made it worse. We haven't had any tea for a week ... the bottom is out of the Universe.' Rudyard Kipling (1865–1936), *Natural Theology*

Tea Gowns and the '*cinq à sept*'

What was a woman to wear for afternoon tea and for the 'at-homes'? The specially designed tea gown, of course. Also known as the 'robe d'interieur', or the 'teagie', the tea gown was a long, flowing dress with wide sleeves based loosely on the Japanese kimono worn by the tea-serving Geishi at tea ceremonies. Anna Maria Russell is credited with introducing them to English society. Nothing is that simple, though: before long there were three distinct types of tea gown, worn depending on the time of day. According to Ella Easton in her *Tea Travels* they were morning wear (undress) for early in the morning, worn in the lady's boudoir rather like a dressing gown; afternoon wear (half dress) worn during the day for the visits of friends or family or for visiting, consisting of a high neckline with long and flowing sleeves; and evening wear (full dress) for dinner parties, which had low necklines with short to almost no sleeves.

> Tea gowns were constructed in several segments, allowing the hostess to change from the lingerie-inspired overtops to the more revealing off-the-shoulder, lower cut silhouette for the evening hours. Fabrics ranged from elaborate gowns with fanciful hand work of embroidery, beading and smocking to the delicate white handkerchief linens accented with pastels.

One of the great benefits of the tea gown was that they could be worn without corsets, thus providing liberation for women to match the new-found freedom of receiving guests for afternoon tea, or going out for tea themselves, by themselves. Evening tea gowns were accessorised with equally elegant gloves, hats, parasols and handbags. For some women the tea gown offered even greater freedoms: with no tiresome corset there was no need for a maid to help in dressing; the tea gown soon gave rise to the French phrase '*cinq à sept*' – the time, between five and seven, when lovers were received in the boudoir and there was no maid to witness the *assignation* ...

For that reason the tea gown was not without its detractors; an angry article was published in *The London World* in 1879 entitled 'Free and Easy Manners in London Society'. It railed,

> Ladies who a few years ago would have considered the idea appalling, calmly array themselves in the glorified dressing-robe known as the 'tea gown' and proceed to display themselves to the eyes of their admirers ... It is absolutely useless, and utterly ridiculous ... At their first beginning the tea gowns only put in an appearance when the beverage from which they take their name was dispensed in the lady's boudoir, and only a rare and favoured specimen of the opposite sex was admitted on sufferance. But such old-fashioned prudery has long been thrown aside ... the tea gowns have descended to the drawing room and the hall ...

For some, tea had a certain sexuality about it. Edward Young's poem 'The Love of Fame, the Universal Passion' was composed in 1725: 'Her two red lips affected Zephyr's blow, / To cool the Bohea, and inflame the Beau.'

Indeed, the fashionistas of the day dictated that 'no season's outfit is considered complete without an assortment of tea gowns' and that as much time and money ought to be spent on them as on an evening dress. The French fashion writer Baroness d'Orchamps had a more dismissive but pragmatic purpose for the tea gown when she suggested it be worn for 'messy chores or for visits to the kitchen'. Furthermore, no

At the other end of the social spectrum: *The Wife at Home* serving teas to the family, from the *British Workman*, 1863.

tea gown ever came cheap, as this 'poem' reveals: 'My lady has a tea-gown / That is wondrous fair to see, – / It is flounced and ruffed and plaited and puffed, / As a tea-gown ought to be; / And I thought she must be jesting / Last night at supper when / She remarked, by chance, that it came from France, / And had cost but two pounds ten.'

Tea Gardens, Tea Dances and Take-Away Tea

To cater for the growing popularity of tea drinking, tea gardens were established from the 1730s as adjuncts of such pleasure gardens as Chelsea's Ranelagh, Marylebone, Covent, Cuper's and Vauxhall in London to allow people to stroll and take tea, the fashionable thing to do. The idea was based on the Dutch 'tavern garden teas'. Sometimes dancing was part of the programme – and so was born the tea dance. Promenading, bowls, gambling, fireworks and concerts added to the entertainment. Handel and a precocious eight-year-old Mozart performed in Ranelagh tea gardens. At the opening of Ranelagh, Horace Walpole said in 1742 that tea gardens attracted anyone who 'loves eating, drinking, staring, or crowding'. Everyone who was anyone went to them, including Henry Fielding and Dr Johnson. Tea gardens gave women one of the first opportunities to frequent mixed public gatherings without slur or criticism. There was, however, some scandal: Lord Nelson apparently met his wife, the already-married Emma Hart, later Lady Hamilton, in a tea garden; she was popularly known as the 'fair tea maker of Edgware Row'.

> '*In vino Veritas. In Aqua satietas. In ...* What is the Latin for Tea? What! Is there no Latin word for Tea? Upon my soul, if I had known that I would have let the vulgar stuff alone.' Hilaire Belloc (1870–1953), *On Tea*

Tea gardens also gave rise to the practice of 'tipping'; there was often some distance between the kitchen and the tea table in the garden, giving the tea time to cool on its journey. To ensure prompt service, and thereby keep the tea hot, each table was equipped with a small wooden box bearing the letters 'TIPS': 'To Insure Prompt Service'. Tea was also served in the afternoon at the bigger, less-refined pleasure gardens where all life congregated. Visitors could relax, drink syllabub, eat cake, go up in a balloon, listen to Handel, or watch a play or fireworks. Pickpockets, 'frail women', sharpers, and other undesirables made up the crowds. Over time, the tea drinking migrated into large hotels and with it went the tea dancing – highly popular until the end of the Second World War and enjoying a revival in the early twenty-first century.

By the early nineteenth century there were something like 200 tea and pleasure gardens in and around London alone. They literally provided a breath of fresh air for a wide section of the population, working class through to aristocracy, and represented one of the first times the classes had mixed socially. William B. Boulton in his *Tea Gardens: An Essay* sums it up perfectly:

It was the citizens of such a town, sober merchants and shopkeepers, apprentices, seamstresses, and artisans who worked continuously, but leisurely and without much stress, during the week and spread themselves over an area of many square miles on Sundays, who formed the chief patrons of the *al fresco* entertainment. The lawyers and military men who filled the chief of the few recognised professions of the last century, supplied their quota of course, and the aristocracy came to most of the *al fresco* entertainments at one time or another, but merely as incidental visitors.

'Peter was not very well during the evening. His mother put him to bed, and made some chamomile, "One table-spoonful to be taken at bed-time".' Beatrix Potter (1866–1943), *The Tale of Peter Rabbit*

The tea gardens at Vauxhall opened as Vauxhall Pleasure Gardens in 1732 and could boast Indian jugglers, a temple, lily ponds, firework displays, gymkhana, balloon flights and supper box pavilions as well as tea. Dubbed the 'Vanity Fair', they were immortalised in Thackeray's novel of the same name. Cuper's Pleasure Gardens in Lambeth was also known as Cupid's Gardens, and could offer an orchestra and fireworks. However, despite its hefty one-shilling entrance fee, it was a magnet for pickpockets and other denizens of the London underworld. In 1753 it was prosecuted under an Act to combat theft in places of public entertainment and the licence was revoked. The owner, a Mrs Evans, continued to run it as an unlicensed tea garden in conjunction with the adjoining Feathers Tavern with evening concerts and fireworks, but it closed in 1760. Ranelagh Gardens in Chelsea had its finest hour when the Venetian Masquerade in honour of the Peace of Aix-la-Chapelle was celebrated there on 26 April 1749; Walpole was delighted:

by far the best understood and prettiest spectacle I ever saw; nothing in a fairy tale even surpassed it ... It began at three o'clock, and about five people of fashion began to go ... In one quarter was a Maypole dressed with garlands and people dancing round it to a tabor and pipes and rustic music, all masqued, as were all the various bands of music that were dispersed in different parts of the garden ... On the Canal was a sort of gondola adorned with flags and streamers, and filled with music, rowing about ... There were booths for tea and wine, gaming tables and dancing, and about two thousand persons. In short it pleased me more than anything I ever saw.

Tobias Smollett in his *Expedition of Humphry Clinker* has the young and upper-class Lydia Melford describe its opulence as

adorned with the most exquisite performances of painting, carving, and gilding, enlighted with a thousand golden lamps, that emulate the noon-day sun; crowded with the great, the rich, the gay, the happy, and the fair; glittering with cloth of gold and silver, lace, embroidery, and precious stones. While these exulting sons and daughters of felicity tread this round of pleasure, or regale in different parties, and separate lodges, with fine imperial tea and other delicious refreshments, their ears are entertained with the most ravishing music, both instrumental and vocal.

Two tea trade cards illustrating the ubiquity of tea drinking in late Victorian times – from society ladies out on their own to picnics with dollies. The brands are Co-operative Wholesale Society tea and Blue Cross tea.

Marylebone was for some a poor man's Vauxhall, while the Paris Garden at Bankside was called [more] 'a foul den than a fair garden'. One anecdote involving Handel and a Dr Fountayne conversing at Ranelagh must rank as one of the greatest faux pas of all time. The composer asked his friend to comment on a new composition being played by the band. Dr Fountayne stiffly proposed that they keep on walking, 'for,' he said, 'it's not worth listening to – it's very poor stuff.' 'You are right, Mr Fountayne,' Handel replied, 'it is very poor stuff. I thought so myself when I had finished it.' So much for 'The Musik for the Royal Fireworks' ... In 1754 Robert Bartholomew advertised his White Conduit House tavern-cum-pleasure garden with the following copy: 'I have completed a long walk, with a handsome circular fish-pond, a number of shady pleasant arbours, enclosed with a fence seven feet high to prevent being the least incommoded from people in the fields; hot loaves and butter every day, milk directly from the cows, coffee, tea, and all manner of liquors in the greatest perfection.'

In 1760 a description of the White Conduit House was published in the *Gentleman's Magazine* no less: '... The red arm'd belle / Here shows her tasty gown, proud to be thought / The butterfly of fashion ... / Tis hurry all / And rattling cups and saucers ... / While tea and cream, and butter'd rolls can please.'

Until 1834 the grounds of the Yorkshire Stingo public house in Marylebone were given over to a bowling green and a tea garden; in 1786, the Committee for the Relief of the Black Poor had distributed alms from there. There were other tea gardens at the spa that was Bagnigge Wells at the present-day King's Cross, 'where ladies and gentlemen may depend on having the best of Tea, Coffee, etc., with hot loaves, every morning and evening'; unfortunately 'it soon fearfully realized the *facilis descensus Averni* ("the descent to Hell is easy"). The gardens were curtailed of their fair proportions, and this once famous resort sank down to a three penny concert-room.' Thomas Keyse was a talented artist who had some of his still-life paintings exhibited at the Royal Academy. Keyse, however, found that tavern-keeping was more profitable, so, in 1765, he bought the Waterman's Arms in Bermondsey, with some land which he converted into a tea-garden. When a chalybeate spring was discovered in the grounds, the Waterman's Arms suddenly became the Bermondsey Spa Gardens, and was redeveloped further with all the accoutrements of a fashionable spa, complemented by the tea garden facilities. Other, imaginatively named, tea gardens included Merlin's Cave, Adam and Eve's Garden, The Three Hats and Finch's Grotto. The life of the pleasure garden was transitory; by 1859 they had all gone, and with them the tea gardens.

'In nothing is the English genius for domesticity more notably declared than in the institution of this festival – almost one may call it so – of afternoon tea. Beneath simple roofs, the hour of tea has something in it of sacred; for it marks the end of domestic work and worry, the beginning of restful, sociable evening. The mere chink of cups and saucers tunes the mind to happy repose.' George Gissing, *The Private Papers of Henry Ryecroft* (1903)

One of the more famous modern tea gardens was the Orchard, opened in Grantchester near Cambridge in 1897. First planted in 1868, the orchard became a tea garden when a group of Cambridge students asked Mrs Stevenson, owner of Orchard House, if she would serve them tea beneath the trees rather than, as was usual, on the front lawn of the house. Popular with students, the home of Rupert Brooke and one of the haunts of members of the Bloomsbury Group (the Grantchester Group, or the Neo-pagans, as Virginia Woolf called them), it attracted such celebrities as Woolf herself, John Maynard Keynes, E. M. Forster, Bertrand Russell, Augustus John, and Ludwig Wittgenstein. Brooke immortalised the place when he wrote *The Old Vicarage, Grantchester* in 1912, ending the poem with that quintessential image of Englishness: 'Stands the church clock at ten-to-three? / And is there honey still for tea?'

The Orchard became a popular venue for early morning breakfasts after many an exhausting May Ball; in 1964, it was so popular that an eight-foot board was erected reminding customers to return their tea cups and saucers in thirty-five different languages. The Orchard, in Brooke's words, was 'Forever England'.

Taking tea was an integral part of the social whirl that took place in the fashionable cities and spa towns of Britain in the eighteenth and nineteenth centuries. In 1757 Mrs Philip Lybbe Powys had the Duke of Devonshire back to her place while in Buxton. When the New Assembly Rooms opened in Bath in 1771 the opening order for crockery included 550 cups and saucers and '100 brown Tea potts'. Tea was found more and more in roadside inns; Viscount Torrington drank it at Bagshot in 1782, in 1785 at Chipping Norton and in 1789 at an inn in Wansford Bridge, in Cambridgeshire. In York the Assembly Rooms were built in 1732 in the Palladian style by Lord Burlington and paid for by subscription to provide the local gentry with somewhere to play dice and cards, dance and drink tea, as featured in Smollett's *The Expedition of Humphrey Clinker*.

Tea dances reached their zenith at the turn of the twentieth century with the Waldorf in Aldwych leading the way in 1908. In 1913 *The Daily Express* reported that 'tango teas are becoming so great a craze' and wondered whether Mrs Average would ever again be content with a quiet cup of tea at home. *The Sunday Times* added that the gowns 'represented the last word in the world of fashion'.

We tend to think of takeaways as modern conveniences; not so – tea-to-go stalls, or breakfasting huts, were a common sight in eighteenth-century towns and cities around England as workers grabbed a cup of tea on the way to the office. One advertisement of the day describes them perfectly: 'This is to give notice to all Ladies and Gentlemen, at Spencer's Original Breakfasting Hut ... may be had every morning except Sundays, fine tea, sugar, bread, butter and milk.'

Teahouses and Tea Rooms

The ubiquity of tea and tea-drinking was well established in Britain by the middle of the eighteenth century; depending on your social standing you could take it at a tea party or in a tea garden or at a pleasure garden, at afternoon tea or at home with high tea, or you could pick up a cup of tea from a breakfasting hut. Two further alternatives existed to cater for the demand that was pouring in from all parts of British society: the teahouse and the tea room. Thomas Twining opened the first known tea room in 1706 at 216 The Strand; it still trades today. In 1787, the company designed its logo, which still decorates its menus and stationery, and is one if the world's oldest commercial logos.

The Aerated Bread Company was founded in 1862 by the social reformer Dr John Dauglish who, disappointed with existing Scottish bread, set about mass producing

Teatime in Wales. The Welsh formed tea clubs, Clwb Te, and pooled resources in times of austerity.

healthy, additive-free breads using a new bread leavening technology: a yeast-free, carbonic acid gas method of bread-making which involved 'nothing but flour, water, a little salt and gas'. The prestigious scientific journal *Nature* later applauded the new technique in an article, 'Aerated Bread', published in 1878: 'As to the perfect cleanliness of this mechanical process for making bread there can be no question; it is immeasurably superior to the barbarous and old, but as Dr. Richardson remarked, *not* "time-honoured" system of kneading dough by the hands and feet of the workman.'

It proved very popular, so the company went a step further and provided somewhere for customers to enjoy this artisan bread, with a cup of tea. One can assume that Dr Dauglish's pursuit of hygiene in his bread-making transferred over to conditions in the teahouses. The self-service ABC teahouse was born in 1864, with the first branch in the courtyard of London's Fenchurch Street station. It was born on the suggestion of a manageress who had been serving free tea and snacks to customers of all classes, and, seeing an opportunity, obtained permission to open a commercial public tea room on the premises. From the company's point of view, ABC could not live by bread alone, so this was a welcome extra revenue stream.

It is unlikely that the manageress received much of a bonus for her innovative, socially progressive idea, or for the extra profits it generated for her company. We have seen how the women's social clubs which sprang up around this time allowed women new freedoms and that one such club was the Somerville above the Mortimer Street ABC. This branch was responsible for yet further social and industrial reform. It turned out that food and refreshments were routinely sent up to the club while ABC staff received no share of the profits in any shape. After complaints, in 1895 the board agreed to provide one hot meal a day at a heavily subsidised price. ABCs soon won a global reputation as safe havens for women; this was evidenced when delegates of the then US-based Congress of the International Council of Women held in London the week of 2 July 1899 were recommended to socialise in ABC teahouses.

ABC teahouses were also responsible for enhanced freedom in women's fashion, and for improving women's health and body image. *The Otago Witness* of December 1908 under its '"Aliens" Letter from England: Fads and Foibles' reported how a waitress at an ABC tea shop died as a result of tight-lacing, the practice where corsets reduced the waist to as small as 17 inches. Her death 'through tight-lacing ... brought the subject of tight-lacing under discussion' and as a consequence, all model gowns were henceforth to have medium waists with an average measurement of an expansive, by comparison, 23 inches. ABC tea shops were an international business, with branches around the world. The Sydney branch was hauled before the courts in 1919 when a woman sued them for £1,000; she claimed she had bitten into an ABC pie and found a dead mouse or rat in it. The article in *The Melbourne Argus*, 'Mouse-in-pie claim fails', reports that the claim was thrown out, adding that the woman had previous records for similar acts of duplicity.

In 1923 there were 250 ABC tea shops, but not everyone liked them; in a prescient article that could have been written today, only aimed at many a different restaurant chain, George Orwell damned the ABC and Lyons' business methods and culture, describing it as a

sinister strand in English catering, the relentless industrialisation that was overtaking it: the 162 tea shops of the Aerated Bread Company, the Lyons Corner

Houses, which rolled out 10 miles of swiss roll every day and manufactured millions of 'frood' (frozen cooked food) meals, the milk bars that served no real food at all ... Everything comes out of a carton or a tin, or is hauled out of a refrigerator or squirted out of a tap or squeezed out of a tube.

Orwell would have been horrified to hear that far worse was still to come. At the other extreme, George Bernard Shaw was an ardent admirer of the ABC teahouse: his diaries tell of frequent visits.

Despite Orwell, the ABC tea shop appears frequently in English literature of the late nineteenth and early twentieth centuries – underlining just how much tea and tea shops were entwined in the fabric of the British way of life. In Bram Stoker's *Dracula* Jonathan Harker stopped by at the local ABC for a cup of tea, after searching for Count Dracula's hideout; in Saki's *The Philanthropist and the Happy Cat* Jocantha Bessbury decides to give a theatre ticket to someone less well off than herself and finds herself in a corner of an ABC tea shop at a table next to a young girl, 'rather plain of feature, with tired, listless eyes and a general air of uncomplaining forlornness'; more corners crop up in Baroness Orczy's 1909 *The Old Man in the Corner*, in which Bill Owen, a 'teahouse detective', meets and talks shop – criminal cases – with a young woman journalist, Miss Polly Burton, in an ABC tea shop:

> Now this particular corner, this very same table, that special view of the magnificent marble hall – known as the Norfolk Street branch of the Aërated Bread Company's depôts – were Polly's own corner, table, and view. Here she had partaken of eleven pennyworth of luncheon and one pennyworth of daily information since her first day in the job.

'The fortune of the celebrated tea men, Forsyte and Treffrey, whose tea, like no other man's tea, had a romantic aroma.' John Galsworthy, *The Forsyte Saga* (1906)

In Dorothy Richardson's *The Tunnel*, Miriam hits on an ABC when deciding where to eat: 'What would you have done?' 'An egg, at an ABC.' 'How fond you are of them ABCs.' 'I love them.' 'What is it you love about them?' 'I think it's their dowdiness. The food is honest; not showy, and they are so blissfully dowdy'.

In Virginia Woolf's 1919 *Night and Day*, Katherine Hilbery goes into an ABC shop to write a letter to Ralph Denham; three years later in her *Jacob's Room*, Florinda walks the streets of London, ending up in an ABC tea shop where she 'read love letters, propping them against the milk pot in the ABC shop; detected glass in the sugar bowl; accused the waitress of wishing to poison her; declared that young men stared at her.'

In Agatha Christie's 1922 *The Secret Adversary* Tommy Beresford, deprived of food and drink, escapes from a spy ring which was planning to wreck the British economy with a general strike, and where is the first place starving Tommy heads for? An ABC tea shop. An ABC tea shop features in A. A. Milne's *The Diary Habit*, where, when editor of *Punch*, he gives an example of how a gripping diary entry should be written:

Tuesday. – Letter from solicitor informing me that I have come into £1,000,000 through the will of an Australian gold-digger named Tomkins. On referring to my diary I find that I saved his life two years ago by plunging into the Serpentine. This is very gratifying. Was late at the office as I had to look in at the Palace on the way, in order to get knighted, but managed to get a good deal of work done before I was interrupted by a madman with a razor, who demanded £100. Shot him after a desperate struggle. Tea at an ABC, where I met the Duke of —. Fell into the Thames on my way home, but swam ashore without difficulty.

'Tea first.' (Wendy's reply to Peter when asked to choose between the Neverland adventure now, or tea.) J. M. Barrie, *Peter Pan* (1911)

Competition for ABC came in the shape of the more upmarket teahouses run by J. Lyons & Co., named after the man chosen to run them, Joseph Nathaniel Lyons. The first teahouse was opened in Piccadilly in 1894, and at one time there were seven in Oxford Street. The first of the famous, larger, West End corner houses opened in 1909 with their distinctive art deco signage and interiors; they occupied sites on the corners of Coventry Street, The Strand and Tottenham Court Road, with Maison Lyonses at Marble Arch and in Shaftesbury Avenue. The Trocadero at Piccadilly, built in 1896, was also a Lyons house. Corner Houses comprised four or five floors. The food hall was on ground level, a delicatessen, with sweets and chocolates, cakes, fruit and flowers; they had hairdressing salons, telephone booths, theatre-booking agencies and offered a twice-a-day food delivery service. The other floors were taken up with themed restaurants each with orchestras and quartets; at one point the Corner Houses were open twenty-four hours a day, with each branch employing around 400 staff. The Coventry Street house could seat 3,000 diners at any one time. Lyons opened what was the largest tea-packing plant in the world at Greenford in Middlesex in 1920. The name of Lyons soon became a by-word for exemplary service and good quality at a reasonable price. The tea, of course, was the best available and the blend used never sold or revealed to the public. They had their own tea estates in Nyasaland (now Malawi). It was Lyons who provided the catering, and tea, for Buckingham Palace garden parties, events at Windsor Castle, London's Guildhall for Lord Mayor's banquets, the Chelsea Flower Shows and Wimbledon. One visitor to the Marble Arch shop recalls how 'the powder room was a sophisticated sanctum with a green leather chesterfield and a pink slot machine that would squirt you with Chanel no 5 for a shilling'. It is enlightening to look back at Lyons' inaugural promotion:

Hitherto there had been nowhere for Mama and the children to have a cup of tea ... prices too had been extortionate ... Lyons introduced ... good cheap food with exceptional smartness and cleanliness; it also gave fresh dignity to the occupation of catering. The new white and gold teashops with their uniformed and attractive waitresses, shone forth in a London drab with drinking dens, dingy coffee houses and 'Slap Bangs'.

We have seen how Lyons contributed to the Second World War effort, providing ration packs as well as tea shops for troops and making bombs. Before the Second World War, tables were serviced by uniformed waitresses known as 'Nippies'. Married women could not be Nippies; the spinster was given her cards when she left to wed. According to *The Picture Post*, every year 800–900 Nippies got married to customers whom they 'met on duty': they wrote that 'being a Nippy is good training for a housewife'. The name was adopted in 1926 to reflect the way in which the girls nipped around the teahouse; before that a Lyons waitress was known as a 'Gladys'. The new name came about through an in-house competition; according to *The Picture Post*, rejected suggestions included 'Sybil-at-your-service', 'Miss Nimble', 'Miss Natty', 'Busy Betty' and even 'Dextrous Doris'. The Nippy became a national icon, symbolic of the girl next door, always approachable and proper; her uniform was spotless and was frequently seen on special occasions and celebrations, worn by little girls emulating the Nippy. The pay for a Nippy in Brighton in 1935 was twenty-six shillings for a fifty-four-hour week with half a crown extra for weekend work; shifts were twelve hours: 11.45 a.m. to 11.45 p.m. The Nippy paid to have her uniform laundered. *Nippy*, a musical, came out in 1930; Margaret Thatcher worked at J. Lyons & Co. in the late 1940s as a research chemist in their Hammersmith laboratories. When not making and serving tea and cakes, Lyons were busy developing and manufacturing Leo, the world's first office computer. In 1951 they financed the University of Cambridge's Electronic Delay Storage Automatic Calculator (EDSAC), the first electronic digital stored-program computer, and built their own programmable digital computer, Leo I, to help with logistics and accounts.

ABC and Lyons were the market leaders, but they were not alone. Lockharts ran fifty coffee rooms in Liverpool and London, while the Express Dairy and Kardomah both

Nippies serving tea to disabled ex-servicemen in the Coventry Street Lyons Corner House.

had their own establishments. Fuller's had their famous Regent Street Tea Rooms and an outlet in the London Coliseum. Europe's most notorious teahouse was surely the Teehaus frequented by Hitler on the Mooslahnerkopf hill across the Obersalzberg valley from the Berghof in the Alps, a round building hidden in the woods.

Less sinister and chilling were the opulent tea rooms opened by the more expensive hotels; they were quick to spot an opportunity to cater for the well-heeled guest, tourist and shopper in that low-revenue period between luncheon and dinner. This nineteenth-century fashion took the tea-taking experience to a different level. Brown's Hotel in London's Albemarle Street has been serving tea in its palatial English tea room since 1837. In the Palm Court at the Ritz Anthony Powell, in his 'Dance to the Music of Time', described an exotic scene there: 'Although stark naked, the nymph looked immensely respectable; less provocative, indeed, than some of the fully dressed young women seated below her.' Lady Diana Cooper remembers the Ritz as the first place women could go unaccompanied without fear of molestation or of causing a scandal.

In addition to hotels, there were, of course, the dedicated tea rooms, springing up in refined and elegant competition. Catherine, or Kate, Cranston (1849–1934) opened her first establishment, the Crown Luncheon Room, in 1878 in Glasgow's Argyle Street. The daughter of a baker and owner of the Edinburgh and Glasgow Railway Chop House and Commercial Lodgings, and brother of a tea dealer who was owner of three tea shops selling tea and sandwiches, Cranston's hallmarks were style, service, quality and hygiene. In 1886 she opened her Ingram Street tea room, decorated in the Arts and Crafts style. She branded her growing chain of tea rooms Miss Cranston's Tea Rooms, opening the famous Willow Tea Rooms designed by Charles Rennie Mackintosh in Sauchiehall Street

Outside the Lyons teahouse in Durban in 1942.

in 1903. Cranston was a key patron of Mackintosh; his distinctive design, right down to the cutlery and waitresses' uniforms, was based on the street outside. 'Saugh' is Scots for a willow tree, and 'haug' a meadow. Rossetti's sonnet 'O Ye, all ye that walk in Willow Wood' was also an influence. 'The Willow' features the 'Room de Luxe' on the first floor, once exclusive to women; this sumptuous room was described at the time as being 'a fantasy for afternoon tea'.

'Those of the younger set ... would sometimes meet in the afternoon in one of their cottages to sip strong, sweet, milkless tea and talk things over. These tea-drinkings were never premeditated ... then someone would say, "How about a cup o' tay?" And they would all run home to fetch a spoonful, with a few leaves over to help make a spoonful for the pot ... this tea-drinking was the woman's hour.' Flora Thompson (1846–1947), *Lark Rise to Candleford*

Bettys Café Tea Rooms

Perhaps the best of all British tea rooms are the six exquisite Bettys, which thrive in four elegant towns in Yorkshire: two in York (St Helen's Square and Stonegate); two in Harrogate (Parliament Street and Harlow Carr); and one each in Georgian Northallerton and Ilkley. Over 2 million customers pass through these six doors every year.

The story of Bettys begins in September 1907, when a twenty-two-year-old Fritz Butzer arrived at King's Cross from Switzerland with no English and little idea of how to reach a town that sounded vaguely like 'Bratwurst'. A job awaited him there. Fritz eventually ended up in Bradford and found work with a Swiss confectioners called Bonnet & Sons in Darley Street – whether Bradford was the original objective and whether Bonnet's was the intended employer is doubtful. Bonnet & Sons paid him the equivalent of 120 Swiss francs per month with free board. Cashing in on the voguishness of all things French, Fritz changed his name to Frederick Belmont. Frederick wasted no time branching out on his own: he opened his first business in July 1919 – a café in Cambridge Crescent in Harrogate on three floors, extravagantly fitted out to the highest standards, 'furnished in grey, with muted pink panels with old-silver borders [and] candleholders'. The china was grey-blue, the coffee and tea pots heavy nickel silver. Day one takings were £30, with £220 for the first week. In 1920 he extended his café, for which takings for the year were £17,000; customers included Lady Haigh, Lord Jellicoe, the Duke of Athlone and Princess Victoria. A bakery was built in Starbeck on the outskirts of Harrogate in 1922, followed by tea rooms in Bradford (in the premises of Bonnets, his first employers) in 1924 and in Leeds in 1930. The York premises opened on 1 June 1937; 'I acquired premises in York, excellent site, best in York for £25,750,' Frederick exults in his diary. York, of course, boasts the famous Belmont Room based on the first class saloon on the *Queen Mary*, on whose maiden voyage to New York Frederick and his wife, Claire, had sailed on the previous year.

In 1962 Bettys acquired Harrogate-based Taylors, founded in 1886 and still makers today of Yorkshire Tea. Their slogan was: 'They came to take our waters; they much prefer our tea.' The teahouse in Valley Gardens was run by Taylors, who also handled

Inside a typical London teahouse in the early twentieth century.

the lucrative catering at the Winter Gardens and at the Royal Spa Concert Rooms. Charles Edward Taylor, a Quaker, and son of a York master grocer, set up the business with 'Kiosk' tea and coffee shops in fashionable Harrogate at 11 Parliament Street and Ilkley after an apprenticeship at James Ashby, the London tea dealers. His time there taught him just how crucial the local water was to particular blends of tea – a lesson well learnt and relevant to this day in the form of Taylor's specially blended Yorkshire Tea for Hard Water. The kiosks were followed by Café Imperials in both towns: Ilkley's opened in 1896; the Harrogate branch in 1907, in the mock baronial castle now occupied by Bettys. The Ilkley Bettys is the old Taylors 'Kiosk' café, and Bettys in Stonegate, York, also occupies the former Taylors 'Kiosk' café.

So who really was Betty? The true identity of Betty has never been revealed and almost certainly never will be. Speculation is rife, however, and there have been many claimants. She may have been the daughter of a doctor who practiced in the building in Cambridge Crescent which was to become the Harrogate Bettys, and who died from tuberculosis; she could have been Betty Lupton, celebrated Queen of the Harrogate Wells from 1778–1838 and chief 'nymph'; she might also have been the actress Betty Fairfax who starred in the West End musical *Betty* around 1915, and to whom Frederick took something of a shine; intriguingly, the musical toured the country and came to Harrogate's Grand Opera House three times between 1916 and 1918. Or, just as plausibly, Betty may be the name of the little girl who brought in a toy tea tray during a meeting at which the name for the new café was being discussed, or of the tea lady who brought in the tea at the tea break ...

During the Second World War Bettys defiantly stayed open and, like other cafés and restaurants, proved resourceful in making a little go a long way. Powdered egg, utility flour, corned beef, spaghetti and beans and all manner of scraps were put to good use. On one occasion Frederick bought a lorry load of honey salvaged from a bombed warehouse and made fudge from it – a rare delicacy in wartime. Occasionally, war brides did not cut their cakes as the cake was nothing more than an iced cardboard box masquerading as a wedding cake. 'Bettys Bar' in York was especially popular with Canadian pilots stationed around York. The famous and poignant 'Bettys Mirror' can still be seen today on the basement floor, the Dive; 500 or so of the 'Bomber Boys' engraved their signatures on the mirror using a diamond ring. Some have returned to see their handiwork, but many of them did not survive the war.

Bettys in Harlow Carr is near to the site of bandstand here, which held frequent pierrot shows. Although the corporation had bought Harlow Moor in 1898, it could not afford the Carr, so this was bought privately for £8,500 by three councillors in 1914, who thus secured the gardens for Harrogate. Harlow Carr is the Royal Horticultural Society's sixty-eight-acre experimental gardens, and features, among many other things, the national collection of rhubarb. The six imposing Doric columns were salvaged from the Harrogate Spa Rooms, which were demolished in 1939.

In 1987 *Punch* paid Bettys a resounding compliment which holds good today: 'For a really good tea it is necessary, naturally, to go to Yorkshire ... Bettys tea rooms provide an example of excellence rarely equalled. The decor is gracious, turn of the century stuff and the waitresses are dressed accordingly in neat black and white. Their attitude to work also owes something to a by-gone age of politeness and decorum.'

British Tea Traditions

A number of enduring, and endearing, tea traditions are woven into the fabric of British society. Cream teas are a speciality in Devon and Cornwall, comprising a pot of tea and scone (not buttered), or a buttered 'split' (a sweet white bread roll) in Cornwall, filled

1-lb. TEA TIN
(½ actual size.)

1-lb. TEA TIN
(½ actual size.)

DECORATED TIN BOXES
designed and printed by
HUDSON SCOTT & SONS, L™·
CARLISLE

2-lb. TEA TIN
(½ actual size.)

Beautifully decorated tea caddies from the 1920s.

A piece of England in Rome: the interior of Babington's Tea Rooms next to the Spanish Steps. It was founded in 1893 by Isabel Cargill and Anne Marie Babington, to cater for the many English-speaking people in Rome when tea in Italy could be bought only in pharmacies.

with generous amounts of strawberry jam and clotted cream. In Devon the jam goes on top, in Cornwall, the other way round. 'Builders' tea is a mug of strong tea, often with sugar, drunk by builders and other craftsmen and workers on their tea break. Removal men drink it constantly: nothing moves without tea. Tea breaks began in the 1800s for factory workers to take refreshment in between clocking-on and dinner time, and halfway through the afternoon. Apparently, office workers today are too busy to stop for tea; they take it back to their desks and get on with their work. Controversy reigns over whether the milk should go in before the tea, or vice versa. The Royal Society of Chemistry has decreed that, for the best results, the milk definitely goes in first. George Orwell, as we shall see, insisted on tea first, while Evelyn Waugh said, 'All nannies and many governesses … put the milk in first,' although this flew in the face of a comment in a letter to Nancy Mitford where he described a mutual acquaintance as 'rather milk in first', meaning a lower-class person. The vast majority of British tea drinkers today drink it in the form of tea bags – an invention which was just about as serendipitous as Shen Nung's discovery of tea in 2737 BC. The tea bag is the descendent of the tea egg and tea ball – metal containers with holes which were filled with loose leaves and plunged into boiling water, and then indecorously hauled out by way of the attached chain. In 1908, New York global tea and coffee merchant Thomas Sullivan began sending samples of tea out in small silken bags. Some recipients believed that these worked like the metal infusers and so immersed the bag into the pot, rather than emptying out the contents, as intended. Result: the tea bag. Conservatism and war delayed the tea bag's invasion of Britain for some fifty years but in 1953 Tetley led the way: in the early 1960s, tea bags then accounted for less than 3 per cent of the British market, now it is nearer 96 per cent.

Tea in English, English in Tea
Because tea has been an everyday part of British life for some 250 years now, it is hardly surprising that tea and tea drinking have found their way into idiomatic English. Here are just a few examples:

Tea and sympathy: kind and empathetic behaviour towards someone who is upset or in trouble.

The phrase derives from the title of a Robert Anderson play of 1953 which addresses the issues faced by a sensitive teenage schoolboy accused of homosexuality at a time when homosexuality was still illegal and homophobia was rife. The 'tea and sympathy' here is provided by the housemaster's wife. The phrase reinforces the association of tea with calming and hospitable behaviour.

'You can't get a cup of tea large enough or a book long enough to suit me.' C. S. Lewis (1898–1963), quoted by Walter Hooper

Storm in a teacup: a fuss over, exaggerating, or excitement about, a trivial matter.

Made famous by the title of a 1937 British film starring Vivien Leigh and Rex Harrison based on the German play *Sturm im Wasserglas* by Bruno Frank. The first use appears to be in 1838 by Catherine Sinclair, the Scottish novelist and children's writer, in her novel *Modern Accomplishments, or the March of Intellect*: 'As for your father's good-humoured jests being ever taken up as a serious affair, it really is like raising a storm in a teacup.' The storm was not always confined to a teacup: there are early English versions which have it raging in a cream bowl (a Duke of Ormond's letter to the Earl of Arlington, 1678) or in a wash-hand basin (*The Gentleman's Magazine*, 1830); sometimes it is a more alliterative 'tempest' (*Blackwood's Edinburgh Magazine*, 1825); Cicero had neither storm nor teacup but he meant the same thing when he said in *De Legibus*, around 52 BC, *Excitabat fluctus in simpulo* or, 'He was stirring up billows in a ladle.' Alexander Pope's *The Rape of the Lock* could be described as 'a storm in a tea cup'; quite fitting, really, since it is set at a tea party.

Just my cup of tea: exactly what I like.

'One's cup of tea' is now synonymous with something good and acceptable. William de Morgan, the Edwardian artist and novelist, was one of the first to use the phrase in his novel *Somehow Good* of 1908, and helped us by explaining its meaning:

'"He may be a bit hot-tempered and impulsive... otherwise, it's simply impossible to help liking him."

To which Sally replied, borrowing an expression from Ann the housemaid, that Fenwick was a cup of tea.

It was metaphorical and descriptive of invigoration.'

Nancy Mitford is the first to record the full phrase, in *Christmas Pudding* from 1932: 'I'm not at all sure I wouldn't rather marry Aunt Loudie. She's even more my cup of tea in many ways.'

Not for all the tea in China: not for anything, no matter how much.

Indicative of the fact that China produces a lot of tea. The *Oxford English Dictionary* considers the phrase to be of Australian origin, from the 1890s. Perhaps they were thinking of J. J. Mann's *Round the World in a Motor Car*, 1914: 'Australia is not a hospitable country for anybody that has not got a white skin ... One is not even allowed to bring in a black servant, and when I applied to the authorities for permission to bring Samand with me, the reply was: "Not for all the tea in China."'

More tea vicar?

A phrase commonly used in comic scenes in plays and television in response to a social faux pas, usually breaking wind. A vicar does not have to be present, neither does a pot of tea. The fact that tea constitutes the phrase is testament again to the ubiquity of tea in British society and that vicars are traditionally offered tea, rather than any other beverage, when they call. Breaking wind is not obligatory when he or she does call.

*

British, and Irish, literature is replete with tea quotations. Time and time again we hear of the cosiness, homeliness and security tea and buttered toast offers; the yearning for tea and for tea-time; the sheer Britishness of it all. It defines our nationhood.

George Orwell, in an article in the *Evening Standard*, 12 January 1946, entitled 'A Nice Cup of Tea', said 'Tea is *one of the mainstays of civilisation in this country* and causes *violent disputes* over how it should be made.' Orwell was a strictly no sugar, tea in first man. He goes on to expatiate on his eleven cardinal points regarding the correct way to make a cup of tea. In his 1936 *Keep the Aspidistra Flying* the illicit evening cup of tea is the highlight of Gordon Comstock's day, the supreme act of defiance against Mrs Wisbech, his landlady, who banned tea drinking in the room, an offence worse even than bringing women in. Tea was Comstock's only concession to bourgeois society: 'Quietly he bolted the door, dragged his cheap suitcase from under the bed, and unlocked it. From it he extracted a sixpenny Woolworth's kettle, a packet of Lyons' tea, a tin of condensed milk, a tea-pot,

'The Tea Shop', from Francis Donkin Bedford's 1899 *Book of Shops*. Catering for all ages, and dogs too.

and a cup. They were all packed in newspaper to prevent them from chinking. He had his regular procedure for making tea. First he half filled the kettle with water from the jug and set it on the oil stove. Then he knelt down and spread out a piece of newspaper. Yesterday's tea-leaves were still in the pot, of course. He shook them out on to the newspaper, cleaned out the pot with his thumb and folded the leaves into a bundle. Presently he would smuggle them downstairs. That was always the most risky part – getting rid of the used tea-leaves. It was like the difficulty murderers have in disposing of the body.'

The most popular recent children's book involving tea drinking is Judith Kerr's *The Tiger Who Came to Tea*, published in 1968. This story involves a friendly tiger who invites himself to tea at Sophie's house and proceeds to eat and drink them out of food and drink. Teatime of course symbolises routine, safety and security for Sophie and, although the tiger is quite harmless and unthreatening, the visit is unpredictable and extraordinary. In 1932 Judith Kerr's father featured on a wanted list by the local Nazi party in Berlin; it has been suggested that the tiger represents the dreaded knock on the door which the Kerr family expected at any time. Judith Kerr's tiger may have been a way in which the author exorcised the ghosts from her past – there again, it may just have been a delightful story about a tiger who came to tea.

Perhaps the most famous play associated with tea is Harold Pinter's *The Tea Party*, which opened at the Duchess Theatre on 17 September 1970; it was adapted from Pinter's own 1963 short story of the same name. A tea party ends the play in which the main character, in a catatonic state, is ignored by the rest of the cast. In 1984 the BBC showed *Threads*, a drama written by Barry Hines about the aftermath of a nuclear war and the resulting nuclear winter in Sheffield. One lady from Suffolk wrote to Margaret Thatcher, Prime Minister at the time, asking her to send a suicide pill which she could take with 'a nice cup of tea' just before the bomb goes off.

In film, one of the most memorable English tea scenes is surely the station refreshment-room sequences in David Lean's 1945 *Brief Encounter*; the screenplay is by Noël Coward, based on his 1936 one-act play *Still Life*. The cups of tea were sipped at fictional Milford Junction, actually a set built at the station at Carnforth. Excerpts from Rachmaninoff's Piano Concerto No. 2 can be heard throughout the film, with a scene in the tea room where an orchestra plays the 'Spanish Dance No. 5 (Bolero)' by Moritz Moszkowski – all lending it that tea room ambience.

'Where there's tea there's hope.' Arthur Wing Pinero (1855–1934)

Other famous tea scenes are in *Mary Poppins* (1965), with her gravity-defying mid-air teatime scene complete with teatime protocol; it is played out to the song 'I Love to Laugh', associating teatime with an uplifting mood and family happiness. In Zeffirelli's 1999 *Tea with Mussolini* a group of expatriate women in 1935 Florence (some of whom are staunchly British) named the Scorpioni are rudely interrupted at their daily ritual afternoon tea by vandalistic fascists. One of their number, Lady Hester, widow of Britain's former ambassador to Italy, arranges a meeting with the dictator, later recounting her 'tea with Mussolini'.

Acute observations on our tea drinking from afar only confirm what we know; one from France, the other from America. In *The Color Purple* (1982), Alice Walker writes, 'Tea to the English is really a picnic indoors.' Robert d'Humieres (1868–1915) describes a visit to Rudyard Kipling in *L'ile et l'empire de Grand-Bretagne: Angleterre, Egypte, Inde*: 'A classic parlour-maid shows me in. Some one is just scrambling off a sofa: Mr Kipling stands before me. He welcomes me charmingly, eagerly: "Tea?" Tea. A hostess of so perfect a distinction that one dare not insist upon it, for fear of displeasing her, presides over this rite of English life.'

We get another French view of the English tea-drinking tradition from Marcel Proust (1871–1922) in his *À la Recherche du Temps Perdu*. Admiration for British culture is one of the themes that underpins the Anglophile Proust's masterpiece; tea drinking plays a key role in this. Tea drinking, it has been argued, is a metaphor for homosexuality in the book. Indeed, in France at the time, *prendre le thé* (to take tea) was slang for 'to have homosexual sex', while *tasse* and *théière* (cup and teapot) were both used to indicate a public convenience frequented by gay men. Emily Welles in her *Proust's Cup of Tea* shows how tea drinking for Proust was quintessentially British and how he used it as an emblem for his love of all things British, including homosexuality.

Tea, of course, features in nursery rhymes, the most famous of which are listed here:

'Polly Put the Kettle On'. Versions exist with Molly taking the lead role. The first record of the rhyme in its modern form is in Dickens' *Barnaby Rudge* (1841). Sukey, in the second verse, is a pet name for Susan, Polly for Mary. Sonny Boy Williamson produced a fine blues version in the 1940s.

> 'The cup of tea on arrival at a country house is a thing which, as a rule, I particularly enjoy. I like the crackling logs, the shaded lights, the scent of buttered toast, the general atmosphere of leisured coziness.' P. G. Wodehouse (1881–1975)

'I'm a Little Teapot': 'I'm a Little Teapot Short and Stout / Here is my Handle here is my Spout ... Just Tip me Up and Pour Me Out ...' The teapot actions are usually priceless and timeless.

Tea features frequently in British popular song, often evoking Britishness itself and the British way of life. 'Tea for Two', one of the most famous tea songs ever, is actually American, originating in the 1925 Broadway musical *No, No Nanette*. 'Everything Stops For Tea' is also American, composed by Maurice Sigler for the 1935 musical *Come Out of the Pantry*, but was performed by Scotsman Jack Buchanan. The song was taken up in the 1940 exhibition by the Ministry of Food when tea was rationed; it was later recorded by blues shouter Long John Baldry. Sting's prim 1987 'I don't drink coffee, I take tea, my dear' from his *Englishman in New York* is based on the life of quintessential exiled Englishman Quentin Crisp. Led Zeppelin's 'Tea for One' (1976) was written by Robert Plant about his nostalgia for England while on one of those endless US tours. Ray Davies is a staunch defender of the English way; in 1967 he wrote, 'Afternoon Tea': 'Tea time won't be the same without my Donna / At night I lie awake and dream of Donna / I think about that small café / That's where we used to meet each day / and then we used to sit a

Taking time out from taking the waters. Elegant Edwardian ladies taking tea in the Taylors pavilion in the Valley Gardens, Harrogate.

while / And drink our afternoon tea.' His 1971 'Have a Cuppa Tea' was also recorded by the Kinks; it regales tea as a panacea and is reminiscent of the disputes over the benefits of tea in the early days: 'If you feel a bit under the weather / If you feel a little bit peeved / Take granny's stand-by potion / For any old cough or wheeze. It's a cure for hepatitis, it's a cure for chronic insomnia / It's a cure for tonsillitis and for water on the knee.' Tea, according to Davies, is to be drunk at any time; it recognises no boundaries – neither political, religious nor racial.

Taking some tea is one of the strategies deployed in wooing Rita, the *lovely* traffic warden, who appears on the Beatles' 1967 *Sergeant Pepper's Lonely Hearts Club Band*. We find Paul McCartney on the same album sleeping in and bedraggled in 'A Day in the Life'; he goes downstairs and drinks 'a cup' ... of tea? The meal that is (high) 'tea' also features: 'Can I bring my friend to tea?' is the question on 'Altogether Now' on *Yellow Submarine* (1969). Getting home for tea is the aim in 'It's All Too Much' on the same album; 'time for tea' and meeting the wife appear on 'Good Morning, Good Morning' on *Sergeant Pepper's*. As a solo artist McCartney recorded 'English Tea' on his 2005 *Chaos and Creation in the Backyard* album; it describes the very English habit of drinking tea, complete with nanny's fairy cakes. 'Would you care to sit with me?' he asks, 'for a cup of English tea? Very twee, very me.' 'Uncle Albert/Admiral Halsey' is a track on McCartney's 1971 *Ram*, which contains the words 'had another look and I had a cup of tea and a butter pie'.

Nothing twee or traditional about the tea mentioned by the Rolling Stones in 'Live with Me' on the 1969 album *Let it Bleed*: 'I got nasty habits/I take tea at three ...' The title song of the same album suggests that they prefer 'coke and sympathy' to tea and sympathy. In 1970 Cat Stevens named an album and a track after tea on his *Tea for the Tillerman*, with fine album artwork showing a tea party for one by Stevens himself. The Who ask 'will you have some tea at the theatre with me?' on the 2006 *Wire and Glass* album, while for Procul Harum 'it was tea-time at the circus' in 1968's *Shine on Brightly*. All very British.

6

Tea Marketing

Five brands dominate the UK tea market: Tetley with a 27 per cent market share, PG Tips (24 per cent), Typhoo (13 per cent), Twinings (11 per cent) and Bettys & Taylors (6 per cent).

With the advent of marketing and advertising in the nineteenth century, packaging, branding and advertising led the way for shoppers to make their own decision in the grocer's as to what to buy, rather than rely on the selection of anonymous teas by the grocer. Horniman's were the first to use packaging with a proprietary name emblazoned on it in 1826, making use of labels that championed the product inside over and above the competition. The refinement of colour printing led to greater opportunities and the rise of the logo.

Advertisements, show cards and posters in particular were often works of art in their own right. The royal family was unofficially enlisted to endorse; patriotism was a key selling point, as were purity and alleged health benefits. Coupons could be exchanged for gifts such as linen, teapots, pianos and pensions. In 1899 *Woman's Weekly* ran a story on this phenomenon: every married woman, it seems, who purchases half a pound of their tea weekly for five consecutive weeks is entitled to a pension of 10s a week in the event of their husband dying, providing he was in good health when she commenced buying the tea, such pension to be continued so long as she remains a widow.

Brooke Bond were the leaders in picture cards, which were inserted into each pack and were highly collectable for their fine illustrations, lucid descriptions and educational value. What mother could deny their children this marvellous learning opportunity? The Co-op had their dividend stamps perforated on their packaging.

Bettys & Taylors

In 1886, Charles Taylor established C. E. Taylor & Son as a tea and coffee importing and blending business in Leeds. Charles soon earned a reputation for quality, winning a gold medal at the London Grocery Exhibition in 1896; he used only the best leaves and made sure his blends complemented the local waters. To sell his teas Charles opened a number of 'Kiosk' coffee shops in Yorkshire towns, and the Café Imperial tea rooms in Ilkley and Harrogate. In 1962 Bettys bought the Taylors business along with their bakeries, cafés and kiosks, including the Café Imperial in Harrogate. This was rebranded as a Bettys Café Tea Room, as were the Taylors Kiosk cafés in Ilkley and York's Stonegate.

Veteran tea-taster and Taylors' last chairman, James Raleigh (1907–1999).

There are over 350 staff at Taylors, handling 200,000 sacks, barrels and chests of tea every year: they buy, taste, blend, pack and ship Yorkshire Tea and other special blends. They import from Sri Lanka to Japan, from Rwanda to Ethiopia – twenty-one countries in all, across three continents. The buyers between them travel to all of these countries, taste up to 1,100 teas in peak Assam buying season and take five years to train, spending twelve months abroad: six months in Africa and six months in India and Sri Lanka, learning how tea is produced and about any problems facing the suppliers. Bettys & Taylors work closely with their tea suppliers, ensuring their blend remains consistent as the seasons affect the volumes and taste of the tea they produce. They also work on climate change mitigation, supporting producers to ensure they can continue to grow their crops into the future. The Tropical House at the tea and coffee factory in Harrogate is full of coffee and cocoa plants. It was Bettys & Taylors who bought the very last lot of tea at the London Tea Auction before its closure on 29 June 1998 – a 44 kg chest of Ceylon Flowery Pekoe. Taylors fought off competition from Twinings, paying £555 per kilo for the lot. The money went to charity, and needless to say, it was the highest amount ever paid for a single chest of tea.

Brooke, Bond & Co.

Brooke Bond & Company was founded by Arthur Brooke in 1845. There was no Mr Bond; the bond is Mr Brooke's word always to provide quality tea. He opened his first tea shop in 1869 in Market Street, Manchester, branching out into wholesale tea sales in the 1870s. Brooke's slogan could be descriptive of any beverage, including alcoholic beverages – 'Good tea unites good company, exhilarates the spirits, banishes restraint from conversation and promotes the happiest purposes of social intercourse' – but it

'When I makes tea I makes tea, as old mother Grogan said. And when I makes water I makes water.' James Joyce (1882–1941), *Ulysses*

This striking Brooke Bond tea card album was one of many produced in the Fifties and Sixties to house the fifty educational cards exquisitely illustrated and avidly collected by girls and boys.

Two of the fine Brooke Bond *Readers' Digest* 'Taking Tea with the World' advertisements from the 1950s. There cannot be many years between the two ads but the copy for India boasts that 'over 100 million cups of Brooke Bond tea are drunk *every day* throughout the world', and by the time we get to Morocco that daily number has rocketed by 50 per cent to over 150 million.

worked. Brooke Bond is famous for the illustrated picture cards inserted in each pack and collected avidly by children – the tea drinkers of the future. The illustrations were top class and were done by famous illustrators such as Charles Tunnicliffe, and the captions on the back were highly informative. Popular series included 'British Wild Animals', 'British Wild Flowers', 'African Wild Life', 'Asian Wild Life', 'Wildlife in Danger' and 'Tropical Birds'.

Horniman's Tea

'Horniman's Tea Company' was founded in 1826 in Newport, on the Isle of Wight, by John Horniman, who moved to London in 1852. Until 1826, the tea market sold only loose leaf teas, thus facilitating the widespread adulteration of tea. Horniman helped put an end to that unscrupulous activity that same year by using machinery to fill packages; the packages had distinctive labels with a proprietary name and were a vehicle for vaunting the superiority of the product inside and, by implication, the inferiority of the competition. It is no accident that by 1891 Horniman's was the biggest-selling tea company in Britain. It is currently owned by Douwe Egberts. John Horniman's other passion was collecting; his ambition was to 'bring the world to Forest Hill' and educate and enrich the lives of those who 'did not have the opportunity to visit distant lands'. The result was the Surrey House Museum, which opened in 1890. It is still open but as the Horniman Museum and Gardens in Forest Hill, with 350,000 items.

'The best thing to do, when you've got a dead body and it's your husband's on the kitchen floor and you don't know what to do about it, is to make yourself a good strong cup of tea.' Anthony Burgess (1917–1993), *One Hand Clapping*

Lipton

Thomas Lipton was a commercial dynamo who made his name in grocery stores – later to become supermarkets. In 1871, having saved up, he bought a shop in Glasgow. By the 1880s he had 200 grocery stores. In 1929 the Lipton business merged with Home & Colonial Stores to form a food group with over 3,000 outlets; changing its name to Allied Suppliers it was acquired by Argyll Foods in 1982, and later rebranded as Presto. The tireless Thomas Lipton travelled the world in search of new lines to stock; he identified tea as a product with a future and, to enable him to sell at a reasonable price by by-passing Mincing Lane, bought his own tea gardens in Ceylon, and packaged and sold Lipton tea. His advertising slogan was 'Direct from the tea gardens to the teapot.' Lipton's were pioneers in some aspects of mass-marketing: in 1914 they sponsored the first flight from Melbourne to Sydney by Maurice Guillaux, the longest air-mail and air-freight flight in the world. Guillaux earned his fee and showed his appreciation by writing, 'I found it the most delicious tea I have ever tasted ... I found it very soothing to the nerves.' Lipton's

Another stunning advertisement, this time for UK Tea Company teas from the 1890s, showing Lilliputian Chinese toiling away to bring the tea to the English tea table: 'From the Palace of Royalty to the Peasant's Cottage.' The three graceful ladies were a trademark of the company, representing Ireland, Scotland and England.

printed 250,000 copies of the letter, obtainable by sending a 1*d* stamp to Lipton's; for a 3*d* stamp, Lipton's sent out a quarter-pound packet of tea. They too were early users of packaging and packing, employing 200 girls in their City Road factory in London. The Lipton Institute of Tea is a tea research centre based in Bedfordshire and owned by Lipton's parent company, Unilever. They had previously opened a tea research farm on Wadmalaw Island. The institute focuses on the psychological and physical health benefits of tea and funds research projects and scientific conferences at academic and research institutions worldwide.

> 'Our trouble is that we drink too much tea. I see in this the slow revenge of the Orient, which has diverted the Yellow River down our throats.' J. B. Priestley, *Observer*, 'Sayings of the Week', 15 May 1949

Mazawattee Tea Company

The Mazawattee Tea Company was at the forefront of the huge expansion of the British tea trade which followed the start of cultivation of tea in India and Ceylon. It was set up by John Boon Densham, who had been an apothecary in Plymouth and was a strict Baptist. His tee-totalism would have influenced his decision to promote and sell tea in 1865 London. The youngest son, John Lane Densham, joined in 1881 and drove the company's growth, adopting the revolutionary retail innovation, introduced in 1826 by John Horniman, of packaging tea so that customers could buy a known brand rather than rely on the grocer's selection of loose tea; the Denshams offered their first packets of Ceylon tea in 1884. John Lane was a keen advocate of branding and advertising; he set about selecting a new name and an image that would sell his tea, coming up with the

Rington's Tea, based in Newcastle, boasting their delivery service and their network of depots throughout the north-east of England from 1907. Today Rington's vans can still be seen delivering tea to the doorstep.

An exquisitely illustrated Lipton's trade card.

exotic 'Mazawattee' in 1887 – a fusion of the Hindi word *mazatha*, meaning luscious, and the Sinhala word *watte(e)*, or garden. The elderly, bespectacled and edentulous grandmother with granddaughter and cup of tea was chosen for adverts and posters, and became very popular, redolent of the warmth and security of home and family. The picture was called 'Old Folks at Home'; their striking advertisements were to appear on every station platform in the British Isles. In 1901 the firm diversified into chocolate, with a new factory in New Cross in which 2,000 people worked. This was an ill-advised move, as indeed was the expansion into retail tea shops. Despite a number of stunts – one of which involved using four zebras to haul the delivery vans in Tunbridge Wells, another being vans with a large Mazawattee tea pot on the roof, through which the exhaust smoke was diverted to come out of the tea pot's spout – the company was on the slide by 1936. Severe damage to the company's buildings in the Blitz did not help; the company, and the name, were sold off in the 1950s.

PG Tips

Also owned by Unilever, PG Tips was launched by Brooke Bond in the 1930s with the name *Pre-Gest-Tee*, claiming that the tea could be drunk before a meal as an aid to digestion. Grocers and salesmen soon abbreviated it to PG. In 1950 PG Tips became the official name; the Tips emphasised the fact that only the tips of the tea plants were used. In Scotland, a special blend of PG sells as Scottish Blend; in Ireland it sells under the Lyons brand. Of all the famous advertisements of PG Tips, perhaps the most enduring and endearing features the slogan '"Dad, do you know the piano's on my foot?" Mr

Above: 1900s tea brands, all showing British patriotism.

Left: One advertising ploy was to promote the amount of duty paid on tea imports, as on this Mazawattee advert; note the all-embracing target market.

Shifter: "You hum it son, I'll play it!"' The TV monkey adverts began in 1956 and were among the first ever broadcast; voice-overs included Peter Sellers, Bruce Forsyth, Kenneth Williams and Bob Monkhouse. The PG Tips chimps are the longest-running characters in British TV advertising, bowing out in 2002. To celebrate their seventy-fifth anniversary PG Tips manufactured the world's most expensive teabag. Commissioned by Boodles the jewellers, it was decorated with 280 diamonds – and raffled off in aid of the Royal Manchester Children's Hospital.

Tetley

In 1822, brothers Joseph and Edward Tetley were selling salt from a pack horse in Yorkshire. They then took on tea and set up as tea merchants Joseph Tetley & Co. in 1837; after moving to London in 1856 they became Joseph Tetley & Company, Wholesale Tea Dealers. Tetley was the first company to sell tea in teabags in the United Kingdom, in 1953. In 1952, Petula Clark's release of 'Anytime Is Tea-Time Now' was used to advertise Tetley tea on Radio Luxembourg. The Tetley Group was bought by India's Tata Group in 2000 for £271 million.

'Make tea, not war.' Monty Python (*c.* 1972)

Twinings

> It seems in some cases kind nature has planned
> That names with their callings agree,
> For Twining the tea-man that lives in the Strand,
> Would be 'wining' deprived of his 'T'.
>
> Thomas Hook (1778–1841)

Twinings have been a force in British tea from its introduction to this country until today. They have grown from Thomas Twining's purchase of Tom's Coffee House at 216 The Strand in 1706. Tea dealer Richard Twining advised William Pitt the Younger on his

A beautifully illustrated Twining's advert from 1899.

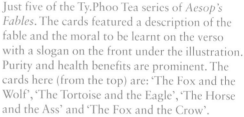

Just five of the Ty.Phoo Tea series of *Aesop's Fables*. The cards featured a description of the fable and the moral to be learnt on the verso with a slogan on the front under the illustration. Purity and health benefits are prominent. The cards here (from the top) are: 'The Fox and the Wolf', 'The Tortoise and the Eagle', 'The Horse and the Ass' and 'The Fox and the Crow'.

Commutation Act, which dramatically lowered the tax on tea in 1784, lobbying for the termination of the East India company monopoly and supplying tea for Red Cross packages, for the Women's Voluntary Service, and for many YMCA wartime canteens during the Second World War. Twinings can boast the world's oldest continually used company logo, from 1787, and is London's oldest rate-payer: Twinings is still serving tea today on the same premises. Jane Austen and Dorothy Wordsworth were customers. The company lays claim to Earl Grey tea, as does former rival Jacksons of Piccadilly, whom Twinings bought in the 1960s. Twinings also bought Belfast-based Nambarrie, a tea company which has been trading since 1860 and is also the third-bestselling brand in Scotland. Much of the company is now based in Wiltshire. During the Blitz in 1940, the company's Tomb Street premises were completely destroyed, leaving only a horse-drawn delivery van intact. 'We [the British] are surely the least quarrelsome of all the nations of the earth and in this the tea-table has undoubtedly played its part ... by the aid of a "nice cup of tea".' Stephen H. Twining.

Ty.Phoo Tea Limited

Typhoo originates in 1903 when Birmingham grocer John Sumner, seeking to alleviate his sister's chronic indigestion, developed and sold a blend of tea in his shop. It worked for sister Mary Augusta; thereafter Sumner focussed on these health benefits in his marketing, claiming that 18,000 doctors recommended his tea:

> Daily do we receive from medical men and women 300 to 700 requests directing us to post samples to their patients'; this is what two of the doctors say: 'I recommend your Ty.phoo tea to many of my patients who are suffering from nervous dyspepsia, and they find it most soothing' and 'Since bringing your Ty.phoo tea to my notice I have drunk no other kind and I find that I have no flatulence now. I have recommended it to all my dyspeptic patients and they all find benefit from its use.

Sumner chose the name because it is derived from the Chinese for 'doctor' and it had an oriental ring to it; 'Tipps' was a typographical error – it should have been 'Tips'. Tea was rooted in the Sumner family: John's grandfather William Sumner published *A Popular Treatise on Tea* in 1863 after going on one of the first London trade missions to China. In 1870, William and John, his father, founded a pharmacy and grocery business in Birmingham.

Select Bibliography

Barr, A., *Drink, A Social History* (London, 1995)

Bennett, A. W., *The World of Caffeine: The Science and Culture of the World's Most Popular Drug* (London, 2001)

Berichevsky, N., *Coffee Or Tea? The Cultural Geography of Consumption* (2008); [http://www.newenglishreview.org/custpage.cfm/frm/9972/sec_id/9972] accessed 08/03/2014.

Bird, P., *The First Food Empire. A History of J. Lyons & Co.* (Chichester, 2000)

Blofeld, J., *The Chinese Art of Tea* (London, 1985)

Brown, P. B., *In Praise of Hot Liquors: The Study of Chocolate, Coffee and Tea-drinking, 1600–1850* (York, 1995)

Browne, J., *Put the Kettle On: The Irish Love Affair with Tea* (Cork, 2013)

Carp, B., *Defiance of the Patriots: The Boston Tea Party and the Making of America* (Yale, 2010)

Chrystal, P., *Chocolate: A History* (London, 2011)

Chrystal, P., *The Rowntree Family: A Social History* (Pickering, 2013)

Crawford, E., *The Women's Suffrage Movement: A Reference Guide 1866–1928* (London 1999)

Crawford, E., *Suffragette Tea from Suffragette China* (2012), [www.womanandhersphere.com/tag/suffragette-tea-rooms]

Easton, E. *Tea Travels – The Afternoon Tea Gown and La Belle Epoque.* [www.oldfashionedliving.com/teagowns], accessed 09/03/2014

Ellis, M., *The Coffee-house: A Cultural History* (London, 2004)

Emerson, R., *British Teapots & Tea Drinking, 1700–1850; illustrated from the Twining Teapot Gallery, Norwich Castle Museum* (London, 1992)

Faulkner, R., *Tea: East and West* (London, 2003)

Ferry, G., *A Computer Called LEO. Lyons Teashops and the World's First Office Computer* (London, 2003)

Forbes, A., *China's Ancient Tea Horse Road* (Chiang Mai, 2011)

Fromer, J., *A Necessary Luxury: Tea in Victorian Britain* (Athens, OH 2008)

Griffiths, J. C., *Tea: The Drink that Changed the World* (London, 2007)

Heiss, M. L., *The Story of Tea: A Cultural History and Drinking Guide* (Berkeley, CA, 2007)

Hobhouse, H., *Seeds of Change: Six Plants that Transformed Mankind* (London, 1999)

Holt, G. ed., *A Cup of Tea: An Afternoon Anthology of Fine China and Tea Trades.* (New York, 1991)

Hopley, C., *The History of Tea* (Barnsley, 2009)

Kinchin, P., *Tea and Taste: The Glasgow Tea Rooms 1875–1975* (Glasgow, 1996)

Lawson, P., *The East India Company: A History* (London, 1993)

Leiper, S., *Precious Cargo: Scots and the China Trade* (Edinburgh, 1997)

Levin, A., 'China Can't Get Enough of this Brew' (Tregothnan Estate), *Daily Telegraph*, 18 May 2013

Mair, V. H., *The True History of Tea* (London, 2009)

Maitland, D., *5000 Years of Tea* (Hong Kong, 2002)

Martin, L. C., *Tea: The Drink that Changed the World* (London, 2007)

Moxham, R., *A Brief History of Tea* (London, 2009)

Pettigrew, J., *Tea and Women – How the Tearoom Supported Women's Suffrage* (6 February 2012) [www.cantonteaco.com/blog/2012/02/tea-and-women-how-the-tearoom-supported-womens-suffrage], accessed 06/03/2014

Pettigrew, J., *A Social History of Tea* (Danville, KY, 2014)

Pitelka, M. (ed.), *Japanese Tea Culture: Art, History, and Practice* (London, 2003)

Pratt, J. N., *Tea Dictionary* (San Francisco, 2010)

Pratt, J. N., *The Ultimate Tea Lover's Treasury* (San Francisco, 2011)

Richardson, B., *The Great Tea Rooms of Britain* (Danville, KY, 2008)

Rose, S., *For all the Tea in China: How England Stole the World's Favorite Drink and Changed History* (New York, 2009)

Saberi, H., *Tea, A Global History* (London, 2010)

Sharma, J., *Empire's Garden: Assam and the Making of India* (Durham, 2011)

Smith, G., *Smuggling in Yorkshire 1700–1850* (Newbury, 1994)

Tanaka, S., *The Tea Ceremony* (Tokyo, 2000)

Thomas, P. D. G., *Tea Party to Independence: The Third Phase of the American Revolution 1773–1776* (Oxford, 1991)

Twining, S., *My Cup of Tea* (London, 2002)

Waley, E., *The Opium War Through Chinese Eyes* (Stanford, CA, 1968)

Walvin, James, *Fruits of Empire: Exotic Produce and British Taste, 1660–1800* (London, 1997)

Weeks, A., *Tea, Rum and Fags: Sustaining Tommy 1914–1918* (Stroud, 2009)

Wharton, K., *Bullets, Bombs and Cups Of Tea: Further Voices of the British Army in Northern Ireland 1969–98* (London, 2012)

Wild, J., *Hearts, Tarts & Rascals: The Story of Bettys* (Harrogate, 2005)

Williams, K., *The Story of Typhoo and the Birmingham Tea Industry* (London, 1990)

Websites

www.tea.co.uk: UK Tea Council

www.bettys.co.uk

www.tregothnan.com: Tregothnan Estate, Truro, Cornwall

www.japanese-tea-ceremony.net

www.indiatea.org

www.tocklai.net: Indian Tea Research Association

www.inttea.com: International Tea Committee. The ITC has been providing the tea industry with valuable statistical information for seventy-five years

www.teausa.org: Tea Association of the USA

www.pouringtea.com: Breda Desplat's fascinating and informative website featuring articles and reviews in tea in Irish history and culture

www.linnean.org/Library-and-Archives/main-library-and-archives: for the Insch Tea Library

www.ceylonteamuseum.com

www.janepettigrew.com: Jane Pettigrew is a leading tea expert, writer and industry consultant. She also runs tea-training courses

www.free2work.org: lists brands which address modern-day slavery

www.teamuse.com: monthly newsletter covering tea-related topics

Acknowledgements

Thanks go to the following who helped in various ways with the book; without them it would be much diminished: Chiara Bedini at Babington's English Tea Rooms, Rome; Lynda Brooks, Librarian and Linnaeus Link Co-ordinator, The Linnean Society of London, for information on the Insch Tea Library; Professor Patricia Lysaght, University College Dublin; Breda Desplat, for help with Irish tea; Professor Markman Ellis, Head of the School of English and Drama, Queen Mary University of London, for permission to quote from the 'QM History of Tea' blog; Sarah Wells at Bettys & Taylors of Harrogate Ltd; Jacqueline Smith at Royal Crown Derby Porcelain Co. Limited for permission to reproduce the teacups on p. 6; Jane Pettigrew for permission to use the images on pages 10 and 60; Adam Eadon at Curious Tea Rooms in Edinburgh.

Index